How foreigners learn Chinese through the PinYin System

汉语入门教程
Elementary Chinese

陈慧玲 著
HUI LING CHEN COMPILED

authorHOUSE®

AuthorHouse™ LLC
1663 Liberty Drive
Bloomington, IN 47403
www.authorhouse.com
Phone: 1-800-839-8640

Published by AuthorHouse   01/07/2014

ISBN: 978-1-4918-4870-8 (sc)
ISBN: 978-1-4918-4869-2 (e)

Library of Congress Control Number: 2014900263

How foreigners learn Chinese through the PinYin System

陈慧玲　著
HUI LING CHEN COMPILED

A Letter of Recommendationor

She is discreet without splurge, prudent without frivolity and practical without fantasy.This is the real portraiture of a girl I knew when I went back to China. She, beautiful and vivacious, later was known the Vice Headmaster of a middle school. Her unique attributes rest with not only the charming beauty,but the summarization of a set of Chinese learning methods available to the westerns through the long teaching. I have lived abroad for 30 years and well known the westerns' difficulties in learning Chinese character and pronunciation. It will be a great help for the westerns to learn the Chinese characters if there is a textbook which can combine and analyze the pronunciation sections of the eastern and western languages to find the similar easy learning methods. As a result, I have suggested her writing a book out of her thirty-year teaching experiences and publishing in America. Easy to understand, the textbook will surely help to promote international cultural exchange.

Mengxiaoyong

道她的職業是一位中學老師，她示同

真是的寫照，她美丽漂亮，後来才知

這是我在回國時訳談的一个女孩子

实際而不幻想，

稳重自制而不輕浮，

言行谨顺而不張揚，

加以进一步的对比，找出相近或差异的掌握

人士学习中国的声调、语音部分

掌握有这样一部教材，把东、西方

方人士学习中国文学的发音的困难，

我在国外生活了三十年，深知西

一套适合西方人学习的汉语的方法。

女人，而且在长期的教学工作中总结

在于她不仅是一位具有吸引力的美丽

的作用。

莲舍对西方人士学习中國的方法，对建设地

語言文学帮助很大。因此，

把三十年的教学经验著书编成画，在

美國出版。这通俗简单易懂的教材，一

莲舍对國际間的文化交流起到帮助

的作用。

（签名）

二〇二三.〇.

中國

A Brief Introduction to the Author

Chen Huiling was born in Qiqihaer City, Heilongjiang Province in 1963 and graduated in 1981 in Teacher-oriented English Major. She has accumulated rich English teaching and teaching management experiences during the teaching of 32 years. Now, as the Vice Headmaster of No.16 Middle School of Qinhuangdao City, Hebei Province, China, she is in charge of teaching. She has builtthe middle school with the advanced teaching and management theories and developed it from an unknown school with only 300 student and staffs into one famous with more than 2000 students and180 staff, receiving the parental praises and social approvals. So she has been commended and awarded many times.

Chen has proposed the modern teaching philosophy, the outstanding teacher plan, and the topping school project from the point of view of an educator and focused on fostering the students' noble personality and comprehensive creativities.

She has convinced the students with her sweet smiles and made intimate friends for her intelligent and elegant qualities. She loves this career and her students more, with the life-long dream of Let Each Student Study in Joy and Teacher Work in Happiness.

As the Vice Headmaster in charge of teaching in the school, she has been studying the differences between English and Chinese teaching, stimulating the students' interest in English learning by various means and solving the Chinese problems in English learning. With the increasing globalization, she is concerned with the foreigners' difficulties and devotes to designing a set of Chinese learning methods available to them. The intersection of the Chinese and foreigners Chinese language learning is the stand of her study.

作者简介

陈慧玲，1963年生于中国黑龙江省齐齐哈尔市，1981年英语师范专业毕业，在32年的教学生涯里，积累了丰富的英语教学与教学管理经验。现任中国河北省秦皇岛市第十六中学副校长，主抓教学工作。在1997年至今十几年期间，用先进的教学理念和先进的管理理念创建了秦皇岛海港区第十六中学，并通过创新和改革使这所学校从一个只有300多名学生和30位教职员工的名不见经传的学校，发展成为一所有2000名学生和180位教职员工的名校，得到了家长的赞扬、社会的认可。多次受到上级行政部门的嘉奖与表彰。

她以教育家的眼光，提出现代教学理念，培养名师，创建名校。培养学生高尚品格和创新能力。

她用美丽的笑容征服了学生，更以知识的优雅气质与学生交知心朋友。她爱这份事业，更爱她的学生。"让每个学生快乐学习，让每个老师快乐工作"，是她追求的目标。

作为中学的一位业务校长，她一直从事英语教学与汉语教学差异的研究，并用多种教学法激发学生学习英语的兴趣，解决了很多中国人存在的各种英语学习问题。随着国际化不断深入，她开始关注外国人学习汉语的难点，并致力于研究一套适合外国人学习汉语的方法。中国人学汉语与外国人学习汉语的交汇点正是她研究的立足点。

Preface

I studied in middle school during the 1970s, when China experienced the Initial Period of Reform and Opening-Up. At that time, there were few accesses to English learning. My father was a doctor, and insisted studying English from the program Chen Lin Broadcasting English every day. He taught me later. Thus, I gradually showed a great interest in English. After graduation from Normal English Department, I became one English teacher, and then a headmaster. I have grown up during the decades of teaching with English which leads to my lifelong career.

Through the years of learning and teaching, I have saved up English learning experiences, summarized a set of practical methods to English learning. I have learned the English International Phonetic Alphabets by means of Chinese Pinyin, and Chinese grammar by means of English Language Structures. The two languages share some identicalnesses and similarities. For example, when we look up in Chinese and English dictionaries, we will do according to the sequence of the 26 English Alphabets. In my opinion, the following are quite important for the Chinese to learn English well:

1. To master the International Phonetic Alphabets and pronounce exactly
2. To accumulate large number of English words and increase oral communications
3. To possess the knowledge of English language structures and rules.
4. To read more English works and know well the general survey of English-speaking countries and their thinking modes.

With the further Reform and Opening, more and more foreigners want to know China and study the Chinese language. From my years of English learning, I have noticed studying Chinese with the help of Transfer. Among the English International Phonetic Alphabets, many alphabets are similar to the Chinese Phonetic Alphabets. The Transfer has obvious effects for the foreign beginners in reading the words correctly and improving their self-taught abilities. From my point of view, the foreigners to study Chinese should know the following two elements: one is the Chinese Pinyin, and the other one is the Chinese Tone. The Chinese tones are fixed, be the First Tone, the Second Tone, the Third Tone and the Forth Tone, just as mā 妈 (mother), má 麻 (sparrow), mǎ 马 (horse) and mà 骂 (abuse). The meanings depend on the changes of the tones. The English is a tonal language, which only conveys the emotions and moods of the speakers. For instance, we will get the distinctive effects and emotive colorings: now (—) shows the calm of the speaker; now (/) expresses the questioning of the speaker " Is it now?"; now (√) tells the speaker does not believe what he hears and demands " Is it really now?"; now (\ ) says the certainty of the speaker "Yes. It is now".

The first step to learn English is to master Pinyin. This book tells foreigners how to learn Chinese in three sections. The first section is how to learn Pinyin by transfering from English international phonetic alphabet to Chinese Pinyin. The second section is to master the spelling of Chinese Pinyin by practicing Pinyin. The third section is to learn the Chinese writing by studying basic strokes.

前 言

　　二十世纪七十年代的中国正处于改革开放前期，当时我正在上中学，在那个年代，学习英语的渠道是很少的。父亲是名医生，他每天坚持跟广播学习英语，我还清楚的记得叫"陈琳广播英语"，父亲学后，再教我。于是，我对英语产生了浓厚的兴趣，师范英语系毕业后，我成为了一名英语老师，又成长为一名校长。几十年的教育生涯里我一直与英语为伴，英语成就了我一生的事业。

　　通过多年的学习与教学，我积累了英语学习的经验，总结出一套实用的学习英语学习方法。我通过"汉语拼音"学会了"英语国际音标"；通过学习"英语的语言结构"掌握了"汉语的语法"。我发现这两种语言之间是有相通或相似之处的。如：在查阅汉语与英语字典时，同样都是按照26个英语字母的顺序进行查阅。

我认为中国人要想学好英语，以下几点是很重要的：

　　1. 一定要掌握国际音标，尤其要读准。

　　2. 掌握大量英语单词，多进行口语交际练习。

　　3. 掌握英语的语言结构，语言规律。

　　4. 大量阅读英语文章，了解英美概况和外国人思维方式。

　　随着中国的改革开放，越来越多的外国人想了解中国，想学习汉语，在多年的学习英语中，我发现可以用"迁移法"来学习汉语。在英语国际音标中，有很多音标与汉语拼音相似，所以"迁移法"对刚刚接触汉语的外国人正确朗读单词和提升自学能力，具有显著的作用。

我认为：外国人学习汉语应该掌握两点（一）汉语拼音，（二）汉语的声调。

汉语的声调是固定的，即一声、二声、三声、四声，如：mā 妈（mother）、má 麻（sparrow）、mǎ 马（horse）、mà 骂（abuse）。语调变了意思就变了。

我认为英语也是有语调的，只不过是用来表示说话人的感情与情绪，如：分别用汉语的四种语调说英语的"now"可有不同效果与不同的感情色彩：其中now（—）表示说话人的心情平静；now（／）表示说话的人在问别人："是现在吗？"，now（√）表示说话人不敢相信自己的耳朵。以为听错了，反问到："真的是现在吗？"now（＼）表示说话人十分肯定，"对！就是现在"。

　　掌握汉语拼音是学好汉语的第一步。本书主要从三个方面教外国人如何学习汉语。第一部分：如何通过"英语国际音标迁移法"学习汉语拼音；第二部分：通过拼音练习，掌握汉字的拼读；第三部分：通过汉字笔画，学习如何书写汉字。

目 录

第一章 英语国际音标"迁移"汉语拼音学习汉语方法介绍

1. 汉语拼音与英语国际音标的对比：

英语共计 48 个音标，20 个元音，28 个辅音，其中 8 个双元音，12 个单元音，元音是组成音节和单词的重要音素，正确的拼读出元音音素的发音，是掌握标准英语发音的关键。

在汉语中有 47 个拼音，其中 6 个单韵母，其作用相当于英语音标中的 12 个单元音，9 个复韵母和 9 个鼻韵母其作用相当于英语音标中 8 个双元音，23 个声母相当于英语音标中的 28 个辅音。准确掌握韵母的发音方法是标准汉语发音的关键。

2. 汉语用的是"前部发音方法"，说话时口腔的前部比较用力，发音位置在口腔的前方。英语用的是"后部发音方法"说话时口腔的后部比较用力，发音位置在口腔的后方。本书通过"英语音标拟音标注法"来学习汉语拼音，通过"音标迁移法"来学习汉语拼音。通过对音标与拼音发音部位的对比，帮助外国人掌握汉语拼音，从而快速的掌握汉语拼音以及拼读汉字的方法。

为了达到"迁移"的目的，本书运用英语国际音标与汉语拼音"音标拟音标注法"教会外国人学习汉语。

读音对比如下：

英语国际音标 "迁移" 汉语拼音学习汉语方法介绍

Section One

An Introduction to the Method of Chinese Learning by Transfering from English International Phonetic Alphabet to Chinese Pinyin

1. Contrast between the Chinese Pinyin and English International Phonetic Alphabet.

There are 48 phonetic alphabets in English with 20 vowels and 28 constants, 20 vowels including 8 double vowels and 12 single vowels. Vowel is the critical phoneme in forming syllable and word and its right reading is the key in studying standard English pronunciation.

There are 47 Chinese Pinyin, 6 simple finals with the same function as the 12 single vowels in English phonetic alphabets, 9 compound finals and 9 nasal finals with the same function as 8 double vowels, and 23 initials just like the 28 constants. The precise sounds of the finals are key in Standard Chinese pronunciation.

2. Chinese pronunciation is termed "Voice Front Approach", that is, the front of the oral cavity exercises more and pronounces. While English pronunciation is termed "Voice Rear Approach", that is, the rear of the oral cavity exercises more and pronounces.

The book will talk about the learning of Chinese Pinyin by Label of English Phonetic Alphabet Sound Symbolism Approach and Phonetic Alphabet Transfer Approach. It will help the foreigners learn the Chinese Pinyin and know the ways to read Chinese characters from the comparison of the places of articulation in phonetic alphabets and Pinyin.

With the purpose of transfer, the book will teach the foreigners to learn Chinese by Phonetic Alphabet Sound Symbolism Approach of the English International Phonetic Alphabets and the Chinese Pinyin.

英语音标与拼音对比总表：

字母表	Aa[ei]　　Bb[bi:]　　Cc[si;]　　Dd[di:]　　Ee[i:]　　Ff[fe]　　Gg[d3i;] Hh[eit§]　　Ii[ai]　　Jj[d3ei]　　Kk[kei]　　Ll[el]　　Mm[em]　　Nn[en] Oo[au]　　Pp[pi:]　　Qq[kju:]　　Rr[a:]　　Ss[es]　　Tt[ti:]　　Uu[ju:] Vv[vi:]　　Ww[dʌblju:]　　Xx[eks]　　Yy[wai]　　Zz[zed]
声母表	b[bə:]　p[pə:]　m[mə:]　f[fə:]　d[də:]　t[tə:]　n[nə:]　l[lə:]　g[gə:] k[kə:]　h[hə:]　j[d3i]　q[t§i]　x[§i]　zh[d3]　ch[t§]　sh[§]　r[3] z[dzi]　c[tsi]　s[si]　y[i:]　w[wu:]
韵母表	a[a:]　o[wə:]　e[ə:]　y[i:]　u[u:]　ü[i:wu]　ai[ai]　ei[ei]　ui[wei] ao[au]　ou[əu]　iu[ju:]　ie[je]　üe[jue]　er[ər]　an[æn]　en[ən] in[in]　un[wən]　ün[jun]　ang[æŋ]　eng[eŋ]　ing[iŋ]　ong[ɔŋ]
整体认读音节	zhi[d3i:]　chi[t§i:]　shi[§i:]　ri[3i:]　zi[dzi:]　ci[tsi:]　si[si:] yi[i:]　wu[wu:]　yu(i:wu)　ye[je]　yue[jue]　yin[i:n]　yun[i:wən] yuan[i:wen]　ying[i:ŋ]

注：汉语、英语对声音的迁移感觉是有差异的。所以，英语的发音我们请教了美、法、德等专家；在迁移音准的校对上，我们请教了日、韩、中等专业人士，尽量做到准确。目的是既适合西方人也要适合于东方人学习。在模仿汉语拼音发音时，要注意模仿口型，体会两种语言发音部位的变化。

3．汉语声调的符号：

　　一声 (-)　　　　二声 (∕)　　　　三声 (√)　　　　四声(\\)

　　一声高高平又平，二声好像上山坡，

　　三声下坡又上坡，四声就像下山坡。

　注：1. 汉语的声调只标在韵母上，标调还要按顺序，i、ü 并列标在 ü 上，轻声上面不标调，i 上标调点要去掉。

2.　当 j、q、x、y 和 ü 相拼时 ü 上面的两点省略不标调。

The comparison of articulation is as the following:

Alphabets	Aa[ei]　Bb[bi:]　Cc[si;]　Dd[di:]　Ee[i:]　Ff[fe]　Gg[d3i;] Hh[eit§]　Ii[ai]　Jj[d3ei]　Kk[kei]　Ll[el]　Mm[em]　Nn[en] Oo[au]　Pp[pi:]　Qq[kju:]　Rr[a:]　Ss[es]　Tt[ti:]　Uu[ju:] Vv[vi:]　Ww[dʌblju:]　Xx[eks]　Yy[wai]　Zz[zed]
Initials	b[bə:]　p[pə:]　m[mə:]　f[fə:]　d[də:]　t[tə:]　n[nə:]　l[lə:] g[gə:]　k[kə:]　h[hə:]　j[d3i]　q[t§i]　x[§i]　zh[d3]　ch[t§] sh[§]　r[3]　z[dzi]　c[tsi]　s[si]　y[i:]　w[wu:]
Finals	a[a:]　o[wə:]　e[ə:]　y[i:]　u[u:]　ü[i:wu]　ai[ai]　ei[ei] ui[wei]　ao[au]　ou[əu]　iu[ju:]　ie[je]　üe[jue]　er[ər] an[æn]　en[ən]　in[in]　un[wən]　ün[jun]　ang[æŋ] eng[eŋ] ing[iŋ]　ong[ɔŋ]
Whole Syllablws	zhi[d3i:]　chi[t§i:]　shi[§i:]　ri[3i:]　zi[dzi:]　ci[tsi:]　si[si:] yi[i:]　wu[wu:] yu(i:wu) ye[je]　yue[jue]　yin[i:n]　yun[i:wən] yuan[i:wen]　ying[i:ŋ]

Note: It is different in the feelings of the sound transfer between the Chinese and English language. So we have consulted the experts of America, France and Germany in the English pronunciation and the professionals of Japan, Republic of Korea and China in checking the intonation of sound transfer in search of accuracy in order to make the book suitable both to the westerns' and easterns' study. When imitating the articulation of Chinese Pinyin, we should pay attention to the mouth shaping tasting the change of the place of articulation in the two languages.

3. The Symbols of the Chinese Tones
the First Tone (-)　the Second Tone (/)
the Third Tone (√)　the Forth Tone (\)
Note:

1. The Chinese tones is only marked on the finals according to the their consequences with i and ü paralledly marked on ü, neutral tone syllable unmarked and i marked without the dot on it.

4

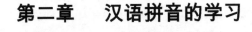

2. When you see j q x y initial goes with ü , you can see u.

第二章 汉语拼音的学习
第一课 单韵母的学习

单韵母的学习：

汉语拼音	英语英音标
a	**/a:/**
o	**/wə/**
e	**/ə:/**
i	**/i:/**
u	**/wu/**
ü	**/i:wu/**

a /a:/ 举例：ā á ǎ à

mā ma	bā ba	mǎ	dà mǐ
词语：妈 妈	爸 爸	马	大 米
mother	father	horse	rice

发音：口张大，舌头放平，嘴唇呈自然状态

区别提示：英语/a:/ 发音时舍身平放在后腔里，舌后靠前的部分用力，发音主要在舌的后部，上下软腭分得很开，两唇张开呈自然，发音稍长。

o /wə/ 举例：ō ó ǒ ò

bō	cài	shā	mò
词语：菠	菜	沙	漠
spinach		desert	

发音：口张开，口型必须是圆圆的，舌尖往后缩

区别提示：汉语拼音中的 o，在英语有两个音组成，/w/和/ə/组成。/w/是摩擦音，/w/是双唇软腭滑动音,舌后部向软腭抬起。双唇呈圆形突出。气流从抬起的后舌与软腭之间的空隙通过，产生摩擦，声带振动。/ə/是中元音，舌头中间部分抬起，舌、唇和牙床都很自然，肌肉相对放松。声带振动。

Section Two   Study of the Chinese Pinyin
Lesson One   Simple Finals

Simple Finals :

Chinese Pinyin	English Phonetic Alphabet
a	/a:/
o	/wə/
e	/ə:/
i	/i:/
u	/wu/
ü	/i:wu/

a   /a:/   e.g. ā á ǎ à

mā ma   bā ba   mǎ   dà mǐ

Words : 妈 妈   爸 爸   马   大 米

mother   father   horse   rice

Articulation: Open the mouth widely with a tongue in horizontal position and lips in natural shaping.

Attention: To make /a:/, put the tongue flat in the back of the oral cavity and the back part near the front of the tongue exercises strongly. The long sound occurs at the back of the tongue with the upper and lower palate in wide open and lips in natural open.

o   /wə/   e.g. ō ó ǒ ò

bō cài   shā mò

Words : 菠   菜   沙   漠

spinach   desert

Articulation: Open the mouth to round with the tip of the tongue withdrawing.

Attention: O in the Chinese Pinyin consists of /w/ and /ə/ in English language.
/w/ is a fricative and a bilabial-velar glide. Raise back of the tongue to the soft palate and round the lips protuberant for the air to run out through .the passage between the back of the tongue and the soft palate with friction. The vocal cords vibrate./ə / is a mid vowel. Raise the center of the tongue with the tongue, lips and gum in natural position and relax the muscle. The vocal cords vibrate.

e   /ə:/   举例： ē é ě è

　　　　　　　　　　tiān é   qì chē   kě lè
　　　　词语： 天 鹅   汽 车   可 乐
　　　　　　　　　swan   bus   coke

发音：双唇自然展开，舌位要平，舌头靠后，舌根稍稍抬高

区别提示：英语/ə:/是中元音，发音时，舌中部向硬腭中部上抬，其高度为中高。舌身与上臼齿有接触，但不紧密。唇形展唇位，展开的程度与/i:/相同，声带振动。

i   /i:/ 举例： ī í ǐ ì

　　　　　　　　　xiǎo jī   xī fāng   qì qiú
　　　　词语： 小 鸡   西 方   气 球
　　　　　　　　chick   West   ballon

发音：上下齿对齐，舌尖抵住下齿龈，嘴角微微张开，让气流通过

区别提示：英语/i:/前元音，舌身前部尽量抬向硬腭，在舌面和硬腭之间留一定的空隙，舌尖抵住前下齿，下颚略向下伸，使牙齿分开。两唇展开，拉向两侧的嘴角，声带振动。

u   /u:/   举例： ū ú ǔ ù

　　　　　　　　　dú shū   shǔ shù
　　　　词语： 读 书   数 数
　　　　　　　read books   count

发音：嘴唇拢圆，向前突出，舌根抬起，舌头后缩。

区别提示：英语/u:/后元音，舌尖离开下齿，舌后部向软腭抬起，在后元音中舌位最高。双唇收圆，向前用力突出，肌肉紧张，成一小孔,声带振动.

ü   /i:wu/   举例： ǖ ǘ ǚ ǜ
　　　　　　　　nǚ hái   lǜ yè   lǚ xíng
　　　　词语： 女 孩   绿 叶   旅 行
　　　　　　　girl   green leaf   travel

发音：口拢圆，舌面向前隆起，口型要比发 u 的音时稍放平一些.

区别提示：汉语拼音中的 ü,在英语有三个音组成，/i:/、/w/和/u 组成。读音时：从/i:/向/wu/滑动组成。

7

e   /ə:/   e.g.   ē   é   ě   è

tiān é   qì chē   kě lè

Words：天 鹅   汽 车   可 乐

swan   bus   coke

Articulation: Open the lips naturally and place the tongue horizontally. Withdraw the tongue and raise the tongue base.

Attention: /ə:/ in English is a mid vowel. To make the sound, raise the center of the tongue to the center of the hard palate to a medial position. The tongue touches the upper molar teeth slightly. Open the lips as /i:/. The vocal cords vibrate.

i   /i:/   e.g.   ī   í   ǐ   ì

xiǎo jī   xī fāng   qì qiú

Words：小 鸡   西 方   气 球

chick   West   ballon

Articulation: Align the upper and lower teeth and push the tip of the tongue against the lower alveolar ridge with the lips opening slightly to let the air out.

Attention: /i:/ in English is a front vowel. To make the sound, raise the front of the tongue to the hard palate as much as possible with a passage between the tongue and the hard palate. Push the tip of the tongue against the front lower teeth with the lower maxilla dropped downward slightly to open the teeth. Spread the lips toward the two sides. The vocal cords vibrate.

u   /u:/   e.g.   ū   ú   ǔ   ù

dú shū   shǔ shù

Words：读 书   数 数

read books   count

Articulation: Round the lips protuberant forward. Raise the tongue base and withdraw the tongue.

Attention: / u:/ in English is a back vowel. To make the sound, move the tip of the tongue apart from the lower teeth and raise the back of the tongue to the soft palate highest. Round the lips forward powerfully with the tense muscle to form a small opening. The vocal cords vibrate.

ü   /i:wu/   e.g.   ǖ   ǘ   ǚ   ǜ

nǚ hái   lǜ yè   lǚ xíng

Words：女 孩   绿 叶   旅 行

girl   green leaf   travel

Articulation: Round the mouth and raise the tongue forward. The mouth shaping is more slightly flat than that of u.

Attention: ü in the Chinese Pinyin consists of three English phonemes, /i:/, /w/ and /u/. The sound is produced by glide from /i:/ to /wu/.

第二课　声母的学习

声母的学习：

汉语拼音	英语英音标
b	/bə:/
P	/pə:/
m	/mə:/
f	/fə:/
d	/də:/
t	/tə:/
n	/nə:/
l	/lə:/
g	/gə:/
k	/kə:/
h	/hə:/
j	/ d3i /
q	//t§i/
x	/§i/
zh	/d3 /
ch	/t§/
sh	/§/
r	/ 3 /
z	/dzi/
c	/tsi/
s	/si/
y	/i:/
w	/wu:/

Lesson Two   Initials

Initials :

Chinese Pinyin	English Phonetic Alphabet
b	/bə:/
P	/pə:/
m	/mə:/
f	/fə:/
d	/də:/
t	/tə:/
n	/nə:/
l	/lə:/
g	/gə:/
k	/kə:/
h	/hə:/
j	/ d3i/
q	//t§i/
x	/§i/
zh	/d3 /
ch	/t§/
sh	/§/
r	/ 3 /
z	/dzi/
c	/tsi/
s	/si/
y	/i:/
w	/wu:/

b　/bə:/　举例：bō　bó　bǒ　bò

　　　　　　　　bō cài　　　　bái tù　　　cǎi bǐ

　　　词语：　菠 菜　　　白 兔　　　彩 笔

　　　　　　　spinach　　　white rabbit　　colour pencil

发音：双唇紧闭，阻碍气流，然后突然放开，不要送气。

区别提示：英语/b/是双唇音，舍身自然放平于口腔中，双唇紧闭，气流挡住在口腔内，在形成一定气流压力之后猛张双唇，气流爆破而出。声带振动。

p　/pə:/　举例：pō　pó　pǒ　pò

　　　　　　　shān pō　　　pán zi　　　pái duì

　　　词语：　山 坡　　　盘 子　　　排 队

　　　　　　　hillside　　　plate　　　form a line

发音：双唇紧闭，阻碍气流，然后突然放开，让气流冲出。

区别提示：英语/p /是双唇音。 舍身自然放平于口腔中，双唇紧闭，气流挡住在口腔内，在形成一定气流压力之后猛张双唇，气流爆破而出。声带不振动。

m　/mə:/　举例：mō　mó　mǒ　mò

　　　mào zi　　huā māo　　　mù tou

　　　词语：　帽 子　　花 猫　　木 头

　　　　　　　cap　　　cat　　　wood

发音：双唇紧闭，气流从鼻孔流出。

区别提示：英语/m/是鼻音、双唇音——舌位：舌身平放在口腔内，双唇紧闭，软腭下垂，气流在口腔内形成一定气压，和发/b/和/p/音时的舌位一样，气流从鼻孔中出来。声带震动。

f　/fə:/　举例：fō　fó　fǒ　fò

　　　　　　　fān chuán　　fēi jī　　　fēng chē

　　　词语：　帆 船　　飞 机　　风 车

　　　　　　　ship　　　plane　　　windmill

发音：上齿接近下唇，形成窄缝，让气流从唇齿之间摩擦挤出,读音

b   /bə:/   e.g.   bō   bó   bǒ   bò

bō cài   bái tù   cǎi bǐ

Words： 菠 菜   白 兔   彩 笔

spinach   white rabbit   colour pencil

Articulation: keep the lips tightly closed to block the air, but then open them to let the air out. Do not release the air. It is not aspirated.

Attention: /b/ in English is a bilabial. Put the tongue naturally flat in the oral cavity. Close the lips tightly to block the air in the oral cavity and open the lips suddenly after there is a certain air pressure. The sound explodes with a strong puff of air. The vocal cords vibrate.

p   /pə:/   e.g.   pō   pó   pǒ   pò

shān pō   pán zi   pái duì

Words： 山 坡   盘 子   排 队

hillside   plate   form a line

Articulation: keep the lips tightly closed to block the air, but then open them suddenly to let the air out.

Attention: /p/ in English is a bilabial. Put the tongue naturally flat in the oral cavity. Close the lips tightly to block the air in the oral cavity and open the lips suddenly after there is a certain air pressure. The sound explodes with a strong puff of air. The vocal cords do not vibrate.

m   /mə:/   e.g.   mō   mó   mǒ   mò

mào zi   huā māo   mù tou

Words： 帽 子   花 猫   木 头

cap   cat   wood

Articulation: keep the lips tightly closed and force the air out through the nose.

Attention: /m/ in English is a nasal and a bilabial. Put the tongue flat in the oral cavity. Close the lips tightly with the soft palate dropped to block the air to a certain pressure. The sound is produced by the air running through the nose with the same tongue position as that of /b/ and /p/. The vocal cords vibrate.

f   /fə:/   e.g.   fō   fó   fǒ   fò

fān chuán   fēi jī   fēng chē

Words： 帆 船   飞 机   风 车

ship   plane   windmill

Articulation: The upper teeth move near to the lower lip to form a narrow passage for the air to be expelled with friction. The sound is shourt and light.

轻短。

区别提示：英语/f /摩擦音、清辅音、唇齿音。上齿轻触下唇。气流从唇与齿之间的空隙通过，唇齿发出摩擦而成。声带：不振动。

d /də:/ 举例： dē   dé   dě   dè

                 huā duǒ   tǔ dì   dú shū

词语：   花 朵   土 地   读 书

              flower   land   read books

发音：舌尖顶住上齿龈，憋住气后突然放开，气流爆发成音。

区别提示：英语/d/齿龈音，舌尖抵住上齿龈，然后放开，让气流爆破而出，双唇微开，吐气较弱，声带振动。

t /tə:/ 举例： tē   té   tě   tè

                 tù zi   táo qì   tài yáng

词语：   兔 子   淘 气   太 阳

             rabbit   naughty   sun

发音：舌头顶住上齿龈，马上后缩往前送气，气流迸出后爆发成音

区别提示：英语/t/齿龈音，舌尖抵住上齿龈，然后放开，使气流爆破而出，双唇微开，吐气较强，声带不振动。

n /nə:/ 举例： nē   né   ně   nè

                 xiǎo niǎo   shuǐ niú   nǎi nai

词语：   小 鸟   水 牛   奶 奶

            lille bird   buffalo   grandmother

发音：舌尖顶住上齿龈后，突然放开，让气流从鼻腔出来。

区别提示：汉语拼音 n 与英语/n/发音基本相同，英语/n/是 鼻音：舌尖抵住上齿龈，软腭下垂，气流从鼻孔中出来。声带震动。

Attention: /f/ in English is a fricative consonant, a voiceless consonant and a labiodental. The upper teeth tough the lower lip slightly with the air running through the passage between them with friction. The vocal cords do not vibrate.

d　　/də:/　e.g.　dē　dé　dě　dè

　　　　　　　　　huā duǒ　　tǔ dì　　dú shū

　　Words：　花　朵　　　土　地　　　读　书

　　　　　　　　flower　　　　land　　　read　books

Articulation: Raise the tongue tip against the upper alveolar ridge to block the air and release it suddenly. The sound explodes with a strong puff of air.

Attention: /f/ in English is a dentialveolar consonant. Raise the tongue tip against the upper alveolar ridge and remove it suddenly with a strong puff, lips parted slightly and air aspirated weakly. The vocal cords vibrate.

t　　/tə:/　　e.g.　　tē　té　tě　tè

　　　　　　　　　tù zi　　　táo qì　　　tài yáng

　　Words：　兔　子　　　淘　气　　　太　阳

　　　　　　　　rabbit　　　naughty　　　sun

Articulation: Raise the tongue against the upper alveolar ridge and withdraw it immediately to release the air forward. The sound explodes with a strong puff of air.

Attention: /t/ in English is a dentialveolar consonant. Raise the tongue tip against the upper alveolar ridge and then remove it to explode with a strong puff of air, lips parted slightly and air aspirated strongly. The vocal cords do notvibrate.

n　　/nə:/　　e.g.　　nē　né　ně　nè

　　　　　　　　　xiǎo niǎo　　shuǐ niú　　nǎi nɑi

　　Words：　小　鸟　　　水　牛　　　奶　奶

　　　　　　　　lille　bird　　buffalo　　grandmother

Articulation: Raise the tongue tip against the upper alveolar ridge and remove it suddenly for the air to run through tha nasal cavity.

Attention: n in the Chinese Pinyin is produced the same as /n/ in English. /n/ in English is a nasal. Raise the tongue tip against the upper alveolar ridge with the soft palate dropped for the air to run through the nostril. The vocal cords vibrate.

l　　/lə:/　举例：lē　lé　lě　lè

　　　　　　　　　　lǐ wù　　　là zhú　　　luò yè

　　　　　词语：礼 物　　　蜡 烛　　　落 叶

　　　　　　　　　gift　　　candle　　　leaf

发音：舌尖翘起顶住上齿龈，嘴唇稍开，舌尖后滑再放开，让气流从舌两侧出来。

　　区别提示：英语/l/ 舌边音,浊辅音、齿龈音。发音时舌尖及舍端紧贴上齿龈，舌前部向硬腭抬起，气流从舍的旁边泄出，声带振动。

g　　/gə:/　举例：gē　gé　gě　gè

　　　　　　　　　gē ge　　　xī guā　　　gǔ tou

　　　　　词语：哥 哥　　　西 瓜　　　骨 头

　　　　　　　　　brother　　watermelon　　bone

发音：舌根隆起，顶住软腭，阻碍气流，然后突然放开，让气流爆发成音。

区别提示：英语/g/是软腭爆破音，舌后位向上升，抵住软腭，然后放开，使气流爆破而出，吐气较弱，双唇自然张开，声带振动。

k　　/kə:/　举例：kē　ké　kě　kè

　　　　　　　　　kē xué　　　shàng kè　　　xīn kǔ

　　　　　词语：科 学　　　上 课　　　辛 苦

　　　　　　　　　science　　have classes　　tired

发音：舌根抬起，顶住软腭，让气流从软腭与舌根中间挤出

区别提示：英语/k/是软腭爆破音，舌后位向上升，抵住软腭，然后放开，使气流爆破而出，吐气较强，双唇自然张开，声带不振动。

h　　/hə:/　举例：hē　hé　hě　hè

　　　　　　　　　hé liú　　　huā duǒ　　　lǎo hǔ

　　　　　词语：河 流　　　花 朵　　　老 虎

　　　　　　　　　river　　　flower　　　tiger

l /lə:/ e.g. lē lé lě lè

  lǐ wù là zhú luò yè

Words : 礼 物 蜡 烛 落 叶

  gift candle leaf

Articulation: Raise the tongue tip against the upper alveolar ridge, open the lips slightly and remove the tip backward for the air to run out from bothsides of the blade.

Attention: /l/ in English is a lateral, a voiced constonant and a dentialveolar. To make the sound, raise the tongue tip against the upper alveolar ridge tightly and the front of the tongue to the hard palate for the air to run out from bothsides of the blade. The vocal cords vibrate.

g /gə:/ e.g. gē gé gě gè

  gē ge xī guā gǔ tou

Words : 哥 哥 西 瓜 骨 头

  brother watermelon bone

Articulation: Raise the tongue base against the soft palate and remove it suddenly. The sound explodes with a strong puff of air.

Attention: /g/ in English is a velar plosive. Raise the back of the tongue against the soft palate and remove it to explode with a strong puff of air, lips parted naturally and air aspirated weakly. The vocal cords vibrate.

k /kə:/ e.g. kē ké kě kè

  kē xué shàng kè xīn kǔ

Words : 科 学 上 课 辛 苦

  science have classes tired

Articulation: Raise the tongue base against the soft palate for the air to be expelled out from the passage between them.

Attention: /k/ in English is a velar plosive. Raise the back of the tongue against the soft palate and remove it to explode with a strong puff of air, lips parted naturally and air aspirated strongly. The vocal cords do not vibrate.

h /hə:/ e.g. hē hé hě hè

  hé liú huā duǒ lǎo hǔ

Words : 河 流 花 朵 老 虎

  river flower tiger

发音：舌根隆起，接近软腭，让气流从软腭与舌根中间摩擦而出

区别提示：英语/h/ 摩擦音,/h/是清辅音、声门摩擦音——舌位：舌身平放于口腔中并使其保持松弛状态。气流：气流通过声门时发生轻微摩擦，然后从口腔中出去。双唇张开，形状随其后面的元音而变化。声带不振动。

j /dʒi/ 举例： jī jí jǐ jì

jù zǐ   jiǎn dāo   jí máng

词语： 句 子   剪 刀   急 忙

sentence   scissors   hurry

发音：上下牙齿靠拢,舌尖抵住下门齿,舌面放松，让气流从齿间通过.

区别提示：汉语拼音中的 j 在英语有二个音组成，/dʒ/和/ i /组成。英语音标/dʒ/是破擦音，/dʒ/是齿龈硬腭摩擦音,舌尖先抵住齿龈形成发/d/的音位，然后舌尖与上齿龈慢慢地分开让气流缓缓地从缝隙中冲出。从发/d/的自然张开的唇形变成略微突出的唇形。声带振动.英语英标/i/是前元音，舌身抬起的高度略低于长元音/i:/,舌尖抵住前下齿，舌尖用力略小于发/i:/时的力度，两齿分开。唇形稍扁。声带振动.(以下不再提及/i /的音)

q / tʂi/ 举例： qī qí qǐ qì

qì qiú   qīng tíng   gāng qín

词语： 气 球   蜻 蜓   钢 琴

balloon   dragonfly   piano

发音：上下齿靠拢,舌面贴住硬腭，让气流冲开舌面的阻碍

区别提示：英语英标/tʂ/是破擦音，/tʂ/是齿龈硬腭摩擦音。先将舌尖抵住上齿龈，不留空隙，形成发/t/的音位，然后舌尖与上齿龈慢慢地分开让气流缓缓地从缝隙中冲出。唇形从/t/的自然张开过渡到ʂ的略微突出的唇形。声带不振动。

x /ʂi / 举例： xī xí xǐ xì

xī guā   xué xí   xià tiān

词语： 西 瓜   学 习   夏 天

watermelon   study   spring

发音：上下齿靠拢,舌面要平，气流从窄缝中挤出，摩擦成声。

Articulation: Raise the tongue base near to the soft palate for the air to be expelled out from the passage

between them with friction.

Attention: /h/ in English is a fricative and a voiceless constonant and a glottal frictive.
Put the tongue flat in the oral cavity and relax it. The air runs out the oral cavity through glottis with a slight friction. The lips open and their shaping changes depending the following vowels. The vocal cords do not vibrate.

j　　/d3i/　　e.g.　jī　jí　jǐ　jì

　　　　　　　　　　jù　zǐ　　jiǎn dāo　　jí　máng

　　Words :　　句　子　　剪　刀　　急　忙

　　　　　　　　　sentence　　scissors　　hurry

Articulation: Narrow the space between the upper and lower teeth, put the tongue tip against the lower incisor and drelax the tongue for the air to run through the passage between the upper and lower teeth.

Attention: / d3/ in English is an affricate and a palato-alveolar fricative. Put the tongue tip against the alveolar ridge to the positon for /d/ and part slowly for the air to run out through the passage, from the natural opening of lips for /d/ to the slightly protuberant opening. The vocal cords vibrate.
/i/ in English is a front vowel. Put the tongue lower than the position of the long vowel /i:/ and the tip against the front lower teeth. It is produced, the upper teeth and lower teeth open, by a smaller strength of the tip than that of the /I:/ with a little flat lip shaping. The vocal cords vibrate. (In the follwong discussion, the sound /i/ will not be talked about any longer.)

q　　/ t§i/　　e.g.　qī　qí　qǐ　qì

　　　　　　　　qì　qiú　　qīng　tíng　　gāng　qín

　　Words :　　气　球　　蜻　蜓　　钢　琴

　　　　　　　　balloon　　dragonfly　　piano

Articulation: Narrow the space between the upper and lower teeth and put the tongue against the hard palate for the air to run over the tongue.

Attention: / t§/ in English is an affricate and a palato-alveolar fricative. Put the tongue tip against the upper alveolar ridge without passage to the positon for /t/ and part slowly for the air to run out through the passage, from the natural opening of lips for /t/ to the slightly protuberant opening for §.The vocal cords do not vibrate.

x　　/§i /　　　　e.g.　xī　xí　xǐ　xì

　　　　　　　　　xī　guā　　xué xí　　xià　tiān

　　Words :　西　瓜　　学　习　　夏　天

　　　　　　　watermelon　　study　　spring

Articulation: Narrow the space between the upper and lower teeth and put the tongue flat for the air to run through the narrow passage with friction.

区别提示：汉语拼音中的 x，在英语有两个音组成，/§/和/i/组成。

英语音标/§/是摩擦音，舌端接近上齿龈后，舌身要向上抬向硬腭，气流从舌和硬腭及上齿龈间的缝隙中通过，发生摩擦音。双唇略突出。声带不震动。

zh /d3/ 举例： zhī zhí zhǐ zhì

xiǎo zhū zhè lǐ zhàn shù

词语： 小 猪 这 里 战 术

pig here tactics

发音：上下齿对齐，舌尖翘起，抵住硬腭前部，让气流从窄缝中出来。

区别提示：英语/ d3/是 破擦音：舌尖先抵住齿龈形成发/d/的音位，然后舌尖与上齿龈慢慢地分开让气流缓缓地从缝隙中冲出。唇形：从发/d/的自然张开的唇形变成略微突出的唇形。声带：振动。

ch /t§/ 举例： chī chí chǐ chì

chūn tiān dǎo chù chē duì

词语： 春 天 到 处 车 队

spring everywhere motorcade

发音：舌尖翘起，抵住硬腭前部，用力送气。

区别提示：英语/t§/ 破擦音。舌位：先将舌尖抵住上齿龈，不留空隙，形成发/t/的音位，然后舌尖与上齿龈慢慢地分开让气流缓缓地从缝隙中冲出。唇形从/t/的自然张开过渡到§的略微突出的唇形。声带不振动。

sh /§/ 举例： shī shí shǐ shì

shòu dàn shā zi lǎo shǔ

词语： 寿 诞 沙 子 老 鼠

birthday sand mouse

发音：舌尖翘起，抵住硬腭前部，气流从窄缝中通过。

区别提示：英语/§/摩擦音，舌端接近上齿龈后，舌身要向上抬向硬腭，气流从舌和硬腭及上齿龈间的缝隙中通过，发生摩擦音，唇形双唇略突出。声带不震动。

Attention: x in the Chinese Pinyin consists of two English phonemes, /§/ and /i/. The English /§/ is a frictive. Put the tongue tip near to the the upper alveolar ridge before raise the tongue to the hard palate to make a passage for the air to run through it with friction. The lips are a little protuberant. The vocal cords do not vibrate.

zh /d3 / e.g. zhī zhí zhǐ zhì

xiǎo zhū   zhè lǐ   zhàn shù

Words： 小 猪   这 里   战 术

pig   here   tactics

Articulation: Align the upper and lower teeth and turn up the tongue tip against the front of the hard palate for the air to run through the narrow passage.

Attention: / d3/ in English is an affricate. Put the tongue tip against the alveolar ridge to the positon for /d/ and then part the tip from the upper alveolar ridge slowly for the air to run out through the passage smoothly, from the natural opening of lips for /d/ to the slightly protuberant opening.. The vocal cords vibrate.

ch /t§ / e.g. chī chí chǐ chì

chūn tiān   dǎo chù   chē duì

Words： 春 天   到 处   车 队

spring   everywhere   motorcade

Articulation: Turn up the tongue tip against the front of the hard palate to aspirate the air powerfully.

Attention: / t§/ in English is an affricate. Put the tongue tip against the upper alveolar ridge without passage to the positon for /t/ and part slowly for the air to run out through the passage, from the natural opening of lips for /t/ to the slightly protuberant opening for §.. The vocal cords do not vibrate.

sh /§/ e.g. shī shí shǐ shì

shòu dàn   shā zi   lǎo shǔ

Words： 寿 诞   沙 子   老 鼠

birthday   sand   mouse

Articulation: Turn up the tongue tip against the front of the hard palate for the air to run through the narrow passage.

Attention: The English /§/ is a frictive. Put the tongue tip near to the the upper alveolar ridge before raise the tongue to the hard palate to make a passage for the air to run through it with friction. The lips are a little protuberant. The vocal cords do not vibrate.

r　/ʒ/　　举例：rī　rí　rǐ　rì

　　　　　　　　fù ráo　　yán rè　　　jī ròu

　　词语：　富 饶　　炎 热　　鸡 肉

　　　　　　abundant　　hot　　　chicken

发音：舌尖抬起，靠近上齿龈，让气流从窄缝中挤出。

区别提示：英语音标/ʒ/是摩擦音，舌端接近上齿龈后部与硬腭前部。双唇突出。声带振动。

z　/dzi/　　举例：zī　zí　zǐ　zì

　　　　　　　　zǔ guó　　　zuò yè　　　zǎo chén

　　词语：　祖 国　　作 业　　早 晨

　　　　　　motherland　　housework　　morning

发音：上下齿对齐，舌尖顶住上齿龈，让气流从窄缝中挤出。

区别提示；英语音标/dz/破擦音，发音时舌前端抵住上齿龈，气流从缝隙中缓缓冲出，自然张开，声带振动。

c　/tsi/　　举例：cī　cí　cǐ　cì

　　　　　　　　cǎi hóng　　　cè liáng　　　cū xīn

　　词语：　彩 虹　　测 量　　粗 心

　　　　　　rainbow　　measure　　careless

发音：舌尖靠近上齿龈，让气流从窄缝中挤出。

区别提示：英语音标英语/ts/破擦音,发音时舌前端抵住上齿龈，气流从缝隙中缓缓冲出，唇形自然张开，声带不振动。

s　/s/　举例：sī　sí　sǐ　sì

　　　　　　　sōng ruǎn　　yán sè　　　bǐ sài

　　词语：　松 软　　颜 色　　比 赛

　　　　　　soft　　　colour　　match

发音：上下齿对齐，舌尖靠近上齿龈，气流通过舌面和上腭间的窄缝．

区别提示：英语/s/是齿龈摩擦音,舌尖接近上齿龈,舌尖与上齿龈之间的距离较小,气流从舌头与硬腭和齿龈之间通过。发生摩擦，声带不振动。

r / ʒ /   e.g.   rī rí rǐ rì

                fù ráo   yán rè   jī ròu

Words :   富 饶   炎 热   鸡 肉

                abundant   hot   chicken

Articulation: Raise the tongue tip near to the the upper alveolar ridge to press the air through the narrow passage.

Attention: The English /ʒ/ is a frictive. Put the tongue tip near to the back of the upper alveolar ridge and the front of tha hard palate with the protuberant lips. The vocal cords vibrate.

z /dzi/   e.g.   zī zí zǐ zì

                zǔ guó   zuò yè   zǎo chén

Words :   祖 国   作 业   早 晨

                motherland   housework   morning

Articulation: Align the upper and lower teeth and turn up the tongue tip against the upper alveolar ridge to press the air through the narrow passage.

Attention: / dz/ in English is an affricate. To make the sound, put the front of tongue against the upper alveolar ridge for the air to run out through the passage smoothly, with the natural opening of lips. The vocal cords vibrate.

c /tsi/   e.g.   cī cí cǐ cì

                cǎi hóng   cè liáng   cū xīn

Words : 彩 虹   测 量   粗 心

                rainbow   measure   careless

Articulation: Turn up the tongue tip near to the upper alveolar ridge to press the air through the narrow passage.

Attention: / ts / in English is an affricate. To make the sound, put the front of tongue against the upper alveolar ridge for the air to run out through the passage smoothly, with the natural opening of lips. The vocal cords do not vibrate.

s /s/   e.g.   sī sí sǐ sì

                sōng ruǎn   yán sè   bǐ sài

Words : 松 软   颜 色   比 赛

                soft   colour   match

Articulation: Align the upper and lower teeth and put the tongue tip near to the upper alveolar ridge for the air to run through the narrow passage between the tongue and the upper maxilla.

Attention: / s / in English is a dentialveolar frictive. Put the tongue tip near to the upper alveolar ridge with a narrow space for the air to run out through the passage of the tongue, hard palate and the alveolar ridge with a friction. The vocal cords do not vibrate.

y /i:/   举例：yī yí yǐ yì

　　　　　　yòu zi　　　yǒng jiǔ　　　yá chǐ

　　词语： 柚 子　　　永 久　　　牙 齿

　　　　　grapefruit　　　forever　　　tooth

发音：发音的部位和方法与发 i 的音基本相同,但比 i 的发音轻短一些。

区别提示：英语/i:/前元音,舌身前部尽量抬向硬腭，在舌面和硬腭之间留一定的空隙，舌尖抵住前下齿，下颚略向下伸，使牙齿分开。两唇展开，拉向两侧的嘴角，声带振动.

w /wu:/   举例：wū wú wǔ wù

　　　　　　qìng wā　　　yú wǎng　　　bàng wǎn

　　词语： 青 蛙　　　渔 网　　　傍 晚

　　　　　frog　　　　net　　　　night

发音：双唇拢圆，向前略突，舌面后部隆起，将气流送出。

区别提示：英语/w /是摩擦音,/w/是双唇软腭滑动音,舌后部向软腭抬起，形成发元音/u:/时的状态。唇形双唇呈圆形突出。气流从抬起的后舌与软腭之间。

第三课　复韵母学习

复韵母学习：

汉语拼音	英语音标
ai	/ai/
ei	/ei/
ui	/wei/
ao	/au/
ou	/əu /
iu	/ju:/
ie	/je/
üe	/jue/
er	/ər/

y /i:/   e.g. yī yí yǐ yì

          yòu zi   yǒng jiǔ   yá chǐ

Words :   柚 子   永 久   牙 齿

          grapefruit   forever   tooth

Articulation: The position and manner of articulation is almost the same for i. but the sound is relative shorter than that of i.

Attention: /i:/ in English is a front vowel. Raise the front of the tongue to the hard palate as much as possible with a passage between the tongue and the hard palate. Push the tip of the tongue against the front lower teeth with the lower maxilla dropped downward slightly to open the teeth. Spread the lips toward the two sides. The vocal cords vibrate.

w /wu:/   e.g. wū wú wǔ wù

          qing wā   yú wǎng   bàng wǎn

Words :   青 蛙   渔 网   傍 晚

          frog   net   night

Articulation: Round the lips protuberant forward and raise back of the tongue ti release the air.

.Attention: /w/ in English is a fricative and a bilabial-velar glide. Raise back of the tongue to the soft palate to the shaping for /u:/. Round the lips protuberant for the air to run out through .the passage between the back of the tongue and the soft palate with friction. The vocal cords vib

Lesson Three   Compound Finals

Compound Finals :

Chinese Pinyin	English Phonetic Alphabet
ai	/ai/
ei	/ei/
ui	/wei/
ao	/au/
ou	/əu /
iu	/ju:/
ie	/je/
üe	/jue/
er	/ər/

ai　/ai/　举例：　āi　ái　ǎi　ài

　　　　　　　　　wǔ tái　　pāi dǎ　　　dà hǎi

　　　　词语：舞 台　　拍 打　　　大 海

　　　　　　　　stage　　　pat　　　　sea

发音：先发 a 的音，逐渐缩小嘴开发 i 的音，且韵尾 i 要发得轻短，

　　　音热连贯，由强到弱。

区别提示：英语/ai /是合口双元音：现将舌身平放在口腔中，起始音是低位前元音/a/，然后滑向放松的高位前元音/i/。舌身由/a/的舌位抬向/i/的方位，这一滑动过程中形成的音便是/ai/。声带振动。

ei　/ei/　举例：　ēi　éi　ěi　èi

　　　　　　　　　cǎo méi　　fēi jī　　　péi bà

　　　　词语：草 莓　　飞 机　　陪 伴

　　　　　　　　strawberry　　plane　　accompany

发音：嘴角向后展开,发 e 的音,并逐渐向 i 的音过渡,i 要发得轻短模糊。

区别提示：英语/ ei/是合口双元音；现将舌尖抵住前下齿，舌高部抬向硬腭，高度为中高，发元音/e/，然后两唇拉向两边，宽度减小，同时舌身高度抬至/I/的高度，在这一滑动过程中形成/ei/音。声带振动。

ui　/ui/.　举例：　uī　uí　uǐ　uì

　　　　　　　　zuǐ ba　　　guì zǐ　　qīng shuǐ

　　　词语：嘴 巴　　柜 子　　清 水

　　　　　　　mouth　　cupboard　　plain water

发音：先发 u 的音，逐渐变成发 i 的音的口型，连贯不中断

区别提示：汉语拼音中的 ui，在英语有两个音组成，/u/和/i/组成。由/u/向/i/滑动。

ao　/au/　　举例：　āo　áo　ǎo　ào

　　　　　　　　　pí bāo　xiǎo dǎo　　tóu nǎo

　　　　词语：皮 包　小 岛　　头 脑

　　　　　　　　bag　　small island　　mind

ai   /ai/   e.g.   āi ái ǎi ài

                   wǔ tái   pāi dǎ   dà hǎi

Words：舞 台   拍 打   大 海

                  stage   pat   sea

Articulation: Begin with the sound of a and then narrow the opening to produce the sound of i. and the Round the lips protuberant forward and raise back of the tongue ti release the air. The syllable coda of i is light and short. The sound is coherent from strong to weak.

Attention: / ai / in English is a closing diphthong. Put the tongue flat in the oral cavity to begin with the front vowel /a/ in a lower position and then glide to the front vowel /i/ in a higher position with the tongue from the position of /a/ to that of /i/. The sound is produced by the glide and the vocal cords vibrate.

ei   /ei/   e.g.   ēi éi ěi èi

                 cǎo méi   fēi jī   péi bà

Words：草 霉   飞 机   陪 伴

             strawberry   plane   accompany

Articulation: Spread the lips backward for the sound of e and gradually change to the sound of i. the latter one is weak short and blurred.

Attention: / ei / in English is a closing diphthong. Put the tongue tip against the front lower teeth and raise the back of the tongue toward the hard palate to a mid-high position to produce the vowel /e/. Then spread the lips to the both sides when raising the tongue to the position of /I/. The sound is produced by the glide and the vocal cords vibrate.

ui   /ui/.   e.g.   uī uí uǐ uì

            zuǐ ba   guì zǐ   qīng shuǐ

Words：嘴 巴   柜 子   清 水

         mouth   cupboard   plain water

Articulation: Begin with the sound of u, and gradually change to the opening of the sound of i. The sound is produced coherently without stop.

Attention: / ui / in the Chinese Pinyin consists of two English phonemes, /u/ and /i/. It is produced by the glide from /u/ to /i/.

ao   /au/   e.g.   āo áo ǎo ào

              pí bāo   xiǎo dǎo   tóu nǎo

        Words：皮 包   小 岛   头 脑

           bag   small island   mind

发音：先发 a 的音，口型逐渐缩小变圆，发 o 的音，连贯不中断。

区别提示：英语/au/合口双元音：/au/的起始音是低位前元音/a/，然后向高位后元音/u/的舌位过渡，此时舌位稍微抬高，口形变小。唇形呈圆形，并向前稍微突出。声带振动。

ou　　/əu/　　举例：ōu　óu　ǒu　òu

　　　　　　　　　　hǎi ōu　　　dòu zi　　　tóu nǎo

　　　　　　　词语：海 鸥　　　豆 子　　　头 脑

　　　　　　　　　　seagull　　　bean　　　mind

发音：先发 o 的音，然后变小口型，双唇突出并拢成小圆形，发出 u 的音，音势要连贯，
　　　一气呵成。

区别提示：英语/əu/ 合口双元音发音规则/əu/是合口双元音——舌位：舌头的口中自然放松，/əu/的起始音是/ə/，发音时向/u/方向过渡，口形也相应地做一些变化。唇形由扁平唇转换为圆唇。声带振动。

iu　　/ju:/　　举例：iū　iú　iǔ　iù

　　　　　　　　　　hé liú　　　pí qiú　　　nǎi niú

　　　　　　　词语：河 流　　　皮 球　　　牛 奶

　　　　　　　　　　river　　　ball　　　milk

发音：先发 i 的音，接着口型由扁到圆，发 u 的音，气流不中断，音热由强到弱。

区别提示：汉语拼音中的 iu，在英语有两个音组成，/j/和 /u:/组成。由/j/向/u:/滑动。英语/j/是 摩擦音，舌前部抬向硬腭，近似法/i:/的舌位。唇形展纯。气流从抬起的舌身与硬腭之间通过，产生摩擦。声带震动。

ie　　/je/　　举例：iē　ié　iě　iè

　　　　　　　　　　jiě jie　　　xié zi　　　qié zi

　　　　　　　词语：姐 姐　　　鞋 子　　　茄 子

　　　　　　　　　　sister　　　shoe　　　eggplant

发音：先发 i 的音，口型张开向 e 的音过渡，音热由弱到强。

区别提示：汉语拼音中的 ie，在英语有两个音组成，/j/和 /e/组成。由/j/向/e/滑动。

Articulation: Begin with the sound of a and narrow to force the lipd into a harrow and round position with only a small opening left to make the sound of o. The sound is produced coherently without stop.

Attention: /au/ in English is a closing diphthong. The sound begins with the front vowel /a/ in a lower position and then change to the back vowel /u/ in a higher position of the tongue. The latter one is narrow with protuberant lips into round position.The vocal cords vibrate.

ou   /əu /   e.g.   ōu   óu   ǒu   òu

　　　　　　　　　hǎi ōu　　　dòu zi　　　tóu nǎo
Words :　海 鸥　　　豆 子　　　头 脑
　　　　　　seagull　　　　bean　　　　mind

Articulation: Begin with the sound of o, and narrow to force the lipd into a harrow and round position with only a small opening left to make the sound of u. The sound is produced coherently without stop.

Attention: / əu / in English is a closing diphthong. Relax the tongue in mouth naturally to begin with /ə/ with a change to /u/ at the same time. The opening is changing correspondingly with flat lips into round lips. The vocal cords vibrate.

iu   /ju:/   e.g.   iū   iú   iǔ   iù

　　　　　　　　　hé liú　　　pí qiú　　　nǎi niú
Words :　河 流　　　皮 球　　　牛 奶
　　　　　　river　　　　ball　　　　milk

Articulation: Begin with the sound of i, and round the lips from a flat position for the sound of u without stop of air from strong to weak.

Attention: iu in the Chinese Pinyin consists of two English phonemes, /j/ and /u:/. It is produced by the glide from /u/ to /i/. /i/ in English is africtive. Raise the front of the tongue toward the hard palate to the similar position for /i:/. Spread the lips for the air to run through the passage between the raised tongue and the hard palate with friction. The vocal cords vibrate.

ie   /je/   e.g.   iē   ié   iě   iè

　　　　　　　　　jiě jie　　xié zi　　qié zi
Words :　姐 姐　　鞋 子　　茄 子
　　　　　　sister　　　shoe　　　eggplant

Articulation: Begin with the sound of i, with the opening changing to the position for e from strong air to weak.

Attention: ie in the Chinese Pinyin consists of two English phonemes, /j/ and /e/. It is produced by the glide from /j/ to /e/.

üe   /jue/   举例：üē üé   üě üè

　　　　　　　　　　xuě rén　　　má què

　　　　词语：　雪　人　　　麻　雀

　　　　　　　　snow man　　　sparrow

发音：先发 ü 的音，马上向 e 的音滑动，口型由圆到扁，音热由强到.

区别提示：汉语拼音中的 üe，在英语有三个音组成，/j/、/u/和 /e/组成。由/j/向/u/ 、/e/滑动。

er   /ər/   举例：ēr ér ěr èr

　　　　　　　　ér zi　　　èr hú　　　　ěr duo

　　　　词语：儿　子　　　二　胡　　　耳　朵

　　　　　　　　son　　　　erhu　　　　　ear

发音：在发 e 的音的同时，舌尖向硬腭卷起，两个拼音字母同时发音。

区别提示：英语/ə/ 中元音：舌头中间部分抬起，舌、唇和牙床都很自然，肌肉相对放松。声带振动。

第四课 鼻音韵母的学习：

鼻音韵母的学习：

汉语拼音	英语音标
an	/æn/
en	/ən/
in	/in/
un	/wun/
ün	/jun/
ang	/æŋ/
eng	/eŋ/
ing	/iŋ/
ong	/oŋ/

üe   /jue/   e.g.   üē   üé   üě   üè

                        xuě   rén   má   qüè

Words：   雪   人   麻   雀

                        snow man   sparrow

Articulation: Begin with the sound of ü and then make a glide to the sound of e with the round opening to the flat position and strong air to weak.

Attention: üe in the Chinese Pinyin consists of three English phonemes, /j/, /u/ and /e/. It is produced by the glide from /j/ to /u/ and /e/.

er   /ər/   e.g.   ēr   ér   ěr   èr

                        ér zi   èr hú   ěr duo

Words：   儿   子   二   胡   耳   朵

                        son   erhu   ear

Articulation: Produce the sound of e and make a retroflex tongue   toward the hard palate at the same time. The two Chinese Pinyin are produced simultaneously.

Attention: /ə/ in English is a central vowel. Raise the mid of the tongue with the tongue, lips and gum in natural position and relax the muscle. The vocal cords vibrate.

Lesson Four   Nasal Finals

Nasal Finals：

Chinese Pinyin	English Phonetic Alphabet
an	/ æn/
en	/ən/
in	/in/
un	/wun/
ün	/jun/
ang	/æŋ/
eng	/eŋ/
ing	/iŋ/
ong	/oŋ/

an   /æn/   举例：ān án ǎn àn

jī dàn   qí gān   shàn zi

词语：   鸡 蛋   旗 杆   扇 子

egg   flagpole   fan

发音：先发 a 的音，然后用舌尖抵住上齿龈,让气流从鼻腔中挤出，滑向 n 的音。

en   /ən/   举例：ēn én ěn èn

shū běn   huā pén   dà mén

词语：书 本   花 盆   大 门

book   flowerpot   gate

发音：先发 e 的音，然后舌尖抬高，让气流从鼻腔发出，滑向 n 的音。

in   /in/   举例：īn ín ǐn ìn

máo jīn   pīn xiě   qīn qiè

词语：   毛 巾   拼 写   亲 切

towel   spell   kind

发音：先发 i 的音，然后舌尖抵住上齿龈，让气流通过鼻腔发出，沿用风吹草动 n 的音。

un   /wun/   举例：   ūn ún ǔn ùn

dūn xià   zhú sǔn   lún chuán

词语：   蹲 下   竹 笋   轮 船

squat   shoots of bamboo   steamship

发音：先发 u 的音，然后舌尖抵住上齿龈，让气从鼻腔发出，滑向 n 的音。

ün   /jun/   举例：yūn yún yǔn yùn

qún zi   xùn liàn   jūn rén

词语：裙 子   训 练   军 人

skirt   train   solider

an /æn/ e.g. ān án ǎn àn

jī dàn   qí gān   shàn zi

Words : 鸡 蛋   旗 杆   扇 子

egg   flagpole   fan

Articulation: Begin with the sound of a and then put the tongue tip against the upper alveolar ridge for the air to be expelled out through the nasal cavity with a glide to the sound of n.

en /ən/ e.g. ēn én ěn èn

shū běn   huā pén   dà mén

Words : 书 本   花 盆   大 门

book   flowerpot   gate

Articulation: Begin with the sound of e and then raise the tongue tip for the air to run out through the nasal cavity with a glide to the sound of n.

in /in/ e.g. īn ín ǐn ìn

máo jīn   pīn xiě   qīn qiè

Words : 毛 巾   拼 写   亲 切

towel   spell   kind

Articulation: Begin with the sound of i and then put the tongue tip against the upper alveolar ridge for the air to run out through the nasal cavity with a glide to the sound of n.

un /wun/ e.g. ūn ún ǔn ùn

dūn xià   zhú sǔn   lún chuán

Words : 蹲 下   竹 笋   轮 船

squat   shoots of bamboo   steamship

Articulation: Begin with the sound of u and then put the tongue tip against the upper alveolar ridge for the air to run out through the nasal cavity with a glide to the sound of n.

ün /jun/ e.g. yūn yún yǔn yùn

qún zi   xùn liàn   jūn rén

Words : 裙 子   训 练   军 人

skirt   train   solider

发音：先发 ü 的音，然后舌尖抵住上齿龈，让气从鼻腔发出，滑向 n 的音。

ang /æŋ/　　举例：āng áng ǎng àng

　　　　　　　　pang xiè　　　shān yáng　　　cāo chǎng

　　　　词语：　螃 蟹　　　山 羊　　　操 场

　　　　　　　　crab　　　　　goat　　　　　playground

发音：先发 a 的音，然后抬高舌位抵住软腭，让气流通过鼻腔，发 ng 的音。

eng /əŋ/　　举例：　ēng éng ěng èng

　　　　　　　　mì fēng　　　tái dēng　　　hán lěng

　　　　词语：　蜜 蜂　　　台 灯　　　寒 冷

　　　　　　　　bee　　　　desk lamp　　　cold

发音：先发 e 的音，然后抬高舌位抵住软腭，让气流通过鼻腔，发 ng 的音。

ing /iŋ/　举例：yīng yíng yǐng yìng

　　　　　　　　bīng gùn　　　píng zi　　　xīng xīng

　　　　词语：　冰 棍　　瓶 子　　星 星

　　　　　　　　popsicle　　　bottle　　　star

发音：先发 i 的音，然后抬高舌位抵住软腭，让气流通过鼻腔，发 ng 的音。

ong /ɔŋ/　　举例：ōng óng ǒng òng

　　　　　　　　shí zhōng　　　gōng rén　　　chóng zi

　　　　词语：　时 钟　　　工 人　　　虫 子

　　　　　　　　clock　　　　worker　　　worm

发音：先发 o 的音，然后抬高舌位抵住软腭，让气流通过鼻腔，发 ng 的音。

Articulation: Begin with the sound of ü and then put the tongue tip against the upper alveolar ridge for the air to run out through the nasal cavity with a glide to the sound of n.

ang   /æŋ/   e.g.   āng áng ǎng àng

páng   xiè   shān   yáng   cāo   chǎng

Words :   螃   蟹   山   羊   操   场

crab   goat   playground

Articulation: Begin with the sound of a and then raise the tongue against the soft palate for the air to run out through the nasal cavity to produce the sound of ng.

eng   /əŋ/   e.g.   ēng éng ěng èng

mì   fēng   tái dēng   hán lěng

Words :   蜜   蜂   台   灯   寒   冷

bee   desk lamp   cold

Articulation: Begin with the sound of e and then raise the tongue against the soft palate for the air to run out through the nasal cavity to produce the sound of ng.

ing   /iŋ/   e.g.   yīng yíng yǐng yìng

bīng   gùn   píng   zi   xīng   xīng

Words :   冰   棍   瓶   子   星   星

popsicle   bottle   star

Articulation: Begin with the sound of i and then raise the tongue against the soft palate for the air to run out through the nasal cavity to produce the sound of ng.

ong   /ɔŋ/   e.g.   ōng óng ǒng òng

shí   zhōng   gōng   rén   chóng   zi

Words :   时   钟   工   人   虫   子

clock   worker   worm

Articulation: Begin with the sound of o and then raise the tongue against the soft palate for the air to run out through the nasal cavity to produce the sound of ng.

第五课 整体认读学习

什么叫整体认读？：1. 直接加上声调，不用拼读，直接读出来。

2. 一般是指添加一个韵母后读音仍和声母一样的音节，也就是指不用拼读即直接认读的音节，所以整体认读音节要直接读出。如： zhi、chi 从声母；yin、yun、ying 从韵母。

汉语拼音	英语音标
zhi	/dʒi: /
chi	/t ʂi:/
shi	/ ʂi:/
ri	/ ʒi:/
zi	/dzi:/
ci	/ tsi:/
si	/si:/
yi	/i:/
wu	/wu:/
yu	/i:wu /
ye	/je/
yue	/jue/
yin	/in/
yun	/iun/
yuan	/iwən/
ying	/i:ŋ/

zhi   /dʒi: /   举例： zhī zhí zhǐ zhì

guǒ zhī   zhí wù   zhǐ zhāng

词语： 果 汁   植 物   纸 张

fruit juice   plant   paper

发音：比单独发 zh 的音更长些，清晰些即可。不能拼读，只能通过声调变化读不同的音。

Lesson Five   Whole Syllables

What is Whole Language Approach?

1. Marke the Chinese Pinyin with tones. Don't spell the syllables and pronounce wholely.

2. A whole syllable refers to one which has the same sound after the initial is combined with a final, that is tosay, which can be read directly without spelling syllables. So a whole syllable is pronounced wholely.

Chinese Pinyin	English Phonetic Alphabet
zhi	/d3i: /
chi	/t §i:/
shi	/ §i:/
ri	/ 3i:/
zi	/dzi:/
ci	/ tsi:/
si	/si:/
yi	/i:/
wu	/wu:/
yu	/i:wu /
ye	/je/
yue	/jue/
yin	/in/
yun	/iun/
yuan	/iwən/
ying	/i:ŋ/

zhi   /d3i: /   e.g.   zhī zhí zhǐ zhì

               guǒ zhī   zhí wù   zhǐ zhāng

Words :   果 汁   植 物   纸 张

              fruit juice   plant   paper

Articulation: It is read longer than the sound of zh, more clearly. In can not be spelt but can be produced variously by the changes of the tones.

chi /t ʂi:/　　举例：　chī　　chí　　chǐ　　chì

chi dào　　　　yá chǐ　　　　chì bǎng

词语：　迟 到　　　　牙 齿　　　　翅 膀

late　　　　　tooth　　　　　wing

发音：比单独发 ch 的音更长些，清晰些即可。不能拼读，只能通过声调变化读不同
的音。

shi / ʂi:/　　举例：　shī　shí　shǐ　shì

lǎo shī　　　shí tou　　　lì shǐ

词语：　老 师　　　石 头　　　历 史

teacher　　　stone　　　　history

发音：比单独发 sh 的音更长些，清晰些即可。不能拼读，只能通过声调变化读不同
的音。

ri / ʒ i/　　举例：　rī　rí　rǐ　rì

rì jì　　　　rì lì　　　　rì chū

词语：　日 记　　　日 历　　　日 出

dairy　　　calendar　　　sunrise

发音：比单独发 r 的音更长些，清晰些。不能拼读，是个特殊的整体音节，读一个
音 ri(日)。

zi /dzi:/　　举例：zī zí zǐ zì

zī liào　　　zǐ sè　　　zì diǎn

词语：资料　　　紫色　　　字典

material　　purple　　dictionary

发音：比单独发 z 的音更长些，清晰些。不能拼读，是个特殊的整体音节，读一个
音。

chi /t ʂiː/　　e.g.　chī　chí　chǐ　chì

　　　　　　　　　chi dào　　　　yá chǐ　　　　chì bǎng

Words :　　迟 到　　　　牙 齿　　　　翅 膀

　　　　　　　late　　　　　tooth　　　　　wing

Articulation: It is read even longer than the sound of ch, more clearly. In can not be spelt but can be produced variously by the changes of the tones.

shi /ʂiː/　　e.g.　shī　shí　shǐ　shì

　　　　　　　　lǎo shī　　　shí tou　　　lì shǐ

Words :　　老 师　　　　石 头　　　　历 史

　　　　　　　teacher　　　　stone　　　　history

Articulation: It is read even longer than the sound of sh, more clearly. In can not be spelt but can be produced variously by the changes of the tones.

ri /ʒi/　　e.g.　rī　rí　rǐ　rì

　　　　　　　　rì jì　　　　rì lì　　　　rì chū

Words :　　日 记　　　日 历　　　日 出

　　　　　　　dairy　　　calendar　　sunrise

Articulation: It is read even longer than the sound of r, more clearly. In can not be spelt but can be produced wholely, as a special whole syllable, ri.

zi /dziː/　　e.g.　zī　zí　zǐ　zì

　　　　　　　　zī liào　　　zǐ sè　　　zì diǎn

Words :　资 料　　　紫 色　　　字 典

　　　　　　　material　　purple　　dictionary

Articulation: It is read even longer than the sound of z, more clearly. In can not be spelt but can be produced wholely, as a special whole syllable.

ci /tsi:/ 　　举例：cī cí cǐ cì

　　　　　　　　 xiá cī 　　　　cí tiě 　　　　bǐ cǐ

　　　　词语：　瑕 疵 　　　 磁 铁 　　　 彼 此
　　　　　　　　 flaw 　　　　magnet 　　　each other

发音：比单独发 c 的音更长些，清晰些。不能拼读，是个特殊的整体音节，读一个音。

si /si:/ 　　举例：sī sí sǐ sì

　　　　　　　　 sī jī 　　　　sǐ bǎn 　　　　sì miào

　　　　词语：　司 机 　　　死 板 　　　 寺 庙
　　　　　　　　 driver 　　　stiff 　　　 temple

发音：比单独发 s 的音更长些，清晰些。不能拼读，是个特殊的整体音节，读一个音。

yi /i:/ 　　举例：yī yí yǐ yì

　　　　　　　　 yī shēng 　　　yí dòng 　　　yǐ zi

　　　　词语：　医 生 　　　 移 动 　　　 椅 子
　　　　　　　　 doctor 　　　move 　　　 chair

发音：比单独发 y 的音更长些，清晰些。不能拼读，是个特殊的整体音节，读一个音。

wu /wu:/ 　　举例：wū wú wǔ wù

　　　　　　　　 wū guī 　　　　wú tóng 　　　　tiào wǔ

　　　　词语：　乌 龟 　　　 梧 桐 　　　 跳 舞
　　　　　　　　 Tortoise 　 Chinese parasol 　　dance

发音：比单独发 w 的音更长些，清晰些。不能拼读，是个特殊的整体音节，读一个音。

ci / tsi:/   e.g.   cī cí cǐ cì

xiá cī   cí tiě   bǐ cǐ

Words : 瑕 疵   磁 铁   彼 此

flaw   magnet   each other

Articulation: It is read even longer than the single sound of c, more clearly. In can not be spelt but can be produced wholely, as a special whole syllable.

si   /si:/   e.g.   sī sí sǐ sì

sī jī   sǐ bǎn   sì miào

Words : 司 机   死 板   寺 庙

driver   stiff   temple

Articulation: It is read even longer than the single sound of s, more clearly. In can not be spelt but can be produced wholely, as a special whole syllable.

yi   /i:/   e.g.   yī yí yǐ yì

yī shēng   yí dòng   yǐ zi

Words : 医 生   移 动   椅 子

doctor   move   chair

Articulation: It is read even longer than the single sound of y, more clearly. In can not be spelt but can be produced wholely, as a special whole syllable.

wu   /wu:/   e.g.   wū wú wǔ wù

wū guī   wú tóng   tiào wǔ

Words : 乌 龟   梧 桐   跳 舞

Tortoise   Chinese parasol   dance

Articulation: It is read even longer than the single sound of w, more clearly. In can not be spelt but can be produced wholely, as a special whole syllable.

yu /i:wu /　　举例： yū　yú　yǔ　yù

yū ní　　　　jīn yú　　　　yǔ máo

词语：　淤 泥　　　金 鱼　　　羽 毛

silt　　　goldfish　　　feather

发音：比单独发 y 的音更长些，清晰些。不能拼读，是个特殊的整体音节，读一个音。

ye /je/　　举例： yē　yé　yě　yè

yē zi　　　　yé ye　　　　tián yě

词语：椰 子　　　爷 爷　　　田 野

coconut　　　grandfather　　　field

发音：比单独发 y 的音更长些，清晰些。不能拼读，是个特殊的整体音节，读一个音。

yue /jue/　　举例： yuē　yué　yuě　yuè

yuē dìng　　yuè liang　　yuè dú

词语：约 定　　月 亮　　阅 读

appointment　　moon　　read

发音：比单独发 üe 的音更长些，清晰些。不能拼读，是个特殊的整体音节，读一个音。

yin /i:n/　　举例： yīn　yín　yǐn　yìn

yīn yuè　　　yín sè　　　yǐn liào

词语：音 乐　　银 色　　饮 料

music　　silver　　drink

发音:比单独发 in 的音稍长即可,不能拼读,只能通过声调变化读不同的音。

yu /i:wu /   e.g.   yū   yú   yǔ   yù

yū ní   jīn yú   yǔ máo

Words：   淤 泥   金 鱼   羽 毛

silt   goldfish   feather

Articulation: It is read even longer than the single sound of y, more clearly. In can not be spelt but can be produced wholely, as a special whole syllable.

ye /je/   e.g.   yē   yé   yě   yè

yē zi   yé ye   tián yě

Words： 椰 子   爷 爷   田 野

coconut   grandfather   field

Articulation: It is read even longer than the single sound of y, more clearly. In can not be spelt but can be produced wholely, as a special whole syllable.

yue /jue/   e.g.   yuē   yué   yuě   yuè

yuē dìng   yuè liang   yuè dú

Words： 约 定   月 亮   阅 读

appointment   moon   read

Articulation: It is read even longer than the single sound of üe, more clearly. In can not be spelt but can be produced wholely, as a special whole syllable.

yin /i:n/   e.g.   yīn   yín   yǐn   yìn

yīn yuè   yín sè   yǐn liào

Words： 音 乐   银 色   饮 料

music   silver   drink

Articulation: It is read even longer than the single sound of in. In can not be spelt but can be produced variously by the changes of the tones.

yun /i:wən/ 举例：yūn　yún　yǔn　yùn

yūn chē　　bái yún　　yǔn xǔ

词　语：晕　车　　白　云　　允　许

carsickness　　cloud　　permit

发音：比单独发ün的音更长些,不能拼读，只能通过声调变化读不同的音。

yuan /i:wen/ 举例：yuān　yuán　yuǎn　yuàn

yuān bó　　yuán xíng　　yuǎn fāng

词　语：渊　博　　圆　形　　远　方

erudite　　round　　far

发音：先发ü的音，口型由扁逐渐张开，滑向an的音，不中断，不能拼读。

ying /i:ŋ/ 举例：yīng　yíng　yǐng　yìng

yīng yǔ　　huān yíng　　yǐng zi

词　语：英　语　　欢　迎　　影　子

English　　welcome　　shadow

yun /i:wən/ e.g.　yūn　yún　yǔn　yùn

yūn chē　　bái yún　　yǔn xǔ

Words：晕　车　　白　云　　允　许

carsickness　　cloud　　permit

Articulation: It is read even longer than the single sound of ün. In can not be spelt but can be produced variously by the changes of the tones.

yuan /i:wen/ e.g.　yuān　yuán　yuǎn　yuàn

yuān bó　　yuán xíng　　yuǎn fāng

Words：渊　博　　圆　形　　远　方

erudite　　round　　far

Articulation: Begin with the sound of ü, and then change the lip from the flat one of into opening gradually, with a glide to the sound of an without stop. It can not be spelt.

ying   /i:ŋ/   e.g.   yīng   yíng   yǐng   yìng

yīng yǔ   huān yíng   yǐng zi

Words :   英 语   欢 迎   影 子

English   welcome   shadow

词汇表 Vocabulary：

mā ma	bā ba	mǎ	dà mǐ	bō cài	shā mò	tiān é	qìchē	kě lè
妈妈	爸爸	马	大米	菠菜	沙漠	天鹅	汽车	可 乐
mother	father	horse	rice	spinach	desert	swan	bus	coke

xiǎo jī	xī fāng	qì qiú	dú shū	shǔ shù	nǚ hái	lǜ yè	lǚ xíng	bái tù
小鸡	西方	气球	读书	数数	女孩	绿叶	旅行	白兔
chick	west	ballon	read books	count	girl	green leaf	travel	white rabbit

cǎi bǐ	shān pō	pán zi	pái duì	mào zi	huā māo	mù tou	fān chuán
彩笔	山坡	盘子	排队	帽子	花猫	木头	帆船
colour pencil	hillside	plate	form line	cap	cat	wood	ship

fēi jī	fēng chē	huā duǒ	tǔ dì	dú shū	tù zi	táo qì	tài yáng
飞机	风车	花朵	土地	读书	兔子	淘气	太阳
plane	windmill	flower	land	read books	rabbit	naughty	sun

xiǎo niǎo	shuǐ niú	nǎi nai	lǐ wù	là zhú	luò yè	gē ge
小鸟	水牛	奶奶	礼物	蜡烛	落叶	哥哥
little bird	buffalo	grandmother	gift	candle	leaf	brother

xī guā	gǔ tou	kē xué	shàng kè	xīn kǔ	hé liú	huā duǒ	lǎo hǔ
西瓜	骨头	科学	上课	辛苦	河流	花朵	老虎
water	bone	science	have class	tired	river	flower	tiger

jù zi	jiǎn dāo	jí máng	qì qiú	qīng tíng	gāng qín
句子	剪刀	急忙	气球	蜻 蜓	钢琴
sentence	scissors	hurry	ballon	dragonfly	piano

xué xí	xià tiān	xiǎo zhū	zhè lǐ	zhàn shù	chūn tiān	dào chù	chē duì
学习	夏天	小猪	这里	战术	春天	到处	车队
study	summer	pig	here	tactics	spring	everywhere	motorcade

shòu dàn	shā zi	lǎo shǔ	fù ráo	yán rè	jī ròu	zǔ guó
寿诞	沙子	老鼠	富饶	炎热	鸡肉	祖国
birthday	sand	mouse	abundant	hot	chicken	motherland

zuò yè	zǎo chén	cǎi hóng	cè liáng	cū xīn	sōng ruǎn	yán sè
作业	早晨	彩虹	测量	粗心	松软	颜色
housework	morning	rainbow	measure	careless	soft	colour

bǐ sài	yòu zi	yǒng jiǔ	yá chǐ	qīng wā	yú wǎng	bàng wǎn
比赛	柚子	永久	牙齿	青蛙	渔网	傍晚
match	grapfruit	soon	tooth	frog	net	night

wǔ tái	pāi dǎ	dà hǎi	cǎo méi	fēi jī	péi bàn
舞台	拍打	大海	草霉	飞机	陪伴
stage	pat	sea	strawberry	plane	accompany

zuǐ ba	guì zi	qīng shuǐ	pí bāo	xiǎo dǎo	tóu nǎo
嘴巴	柜子	清水	皮包	小岛	头脑
mouth	cupboard	plain water	bag	small island	mind

hǎi ōu	dòu zi	tóu nǎo	hé liú	pí qiú	niú nǎi
海鸥	豆子	头脑	河流	皮球	牛奶
seagull	bean	brain	river	ball	milk

jiě jie	xié zi	qié zi	xuě rén	má què	ér zi	èr hú
姐姐	鞋子	茄子	雪人	麻雀	儿子	二胡
sister	shoe	eggplant	snow man	sparrow	son	erhu

ěr duǒ	jī dàn	qí gān	shàn zi	shū běn	huā pén	dà mén
耳朵	鸡蛋	旗杆	扇子	书本	花盆	大门
ear	egg	flagpole	fan	book	flowerpot	gate

máo jīn	pīn xiě	qīn qiè	dūn xià	zhú sǔn	lún chuán
毛巾	拼写	亲切	蹲下	竹笋	轮船
towel	spell	kind	squat	shoots of bamboo	steamship

qún zi	xùn liàn	jūn rén	páng xiè	shān yáng	cāo chǎng
裙子	训练	军人	螃蟹	山羊	操场
skirt	train	solider	crab	goat	playground

mì fēng	tái dēng	hán lěng	bīng gùn	píng zi	xīng xing
蜜蜂	台灯	寒冷	冰棍	瓶子	星星
bee	desk lamp	cold	popscile	bollte	star

shí zhōng	gōng rén	chóng zi	guǒ zhī	zhí wù	zhǐ zhāng
时钟	工人	虫子	果汁	植物	纸张
clock	worker	worm	fruit juice	plant	paper

lǎo shī	shí tou	lì shǐ	rì jì	rì lì	rì chū
老师	石头	历史	日记	日历	日出
teacher	stone	history	dairy	calendar	sunrise

zī liào	zǐ sè	zì diǎn	xiá cī	cí tiě	bǐ cǐ
资料	紫色	字典	瑕疵	磁铁	彼此
material	purple	dictionary	flaw	magnet	each othe

sī jī	sǐ bǎn	sì miào	yī shēng	yí dòng	yǐ zi
司机	死板	寺庙	医生	移动	椅子
driver	stiff	temple	doctor	move	chair

wū guī	wú tóng	tiào wǔ	yū ní	jīn yú	yǔ máo
乌龟	梧桐	跳舞	淤泥	金鱼	羽毛
tortoise	Chinese parasol	dance	silt	goldfish	feather

yē zi	yé ye	tián yě	yuē dìng	yuè liang	yuè dú
椰子	爷爷	田野	约定	月亮	阅读
coconut	grandfather	field	appointment	moon	read

yīn yuè	yín sè	yǐn liào	yùn chē	bái yún	yǔn xǔ
音乐	银色	饮料	晕车	白云	允许
music	silver	drink	carsickness	cloud	permit

yuān bó	yuán xíng	yuǎn fāng	yīng yǔ	huān yíng	yǐng zi
渊博	圆形	远方	英语	欢迎	影子
erudite	round	far	English	welcome	shadow

第三章 学习拼读汉字

Section Three Learn to Spell the Chinese Characters

第一课：日常汉语

Lesson One：Everyday English

1、 家庭及其他成员（包括职业）

Family and Members (vocation included)

宝宝	b-ǎo b-ao	baby
男孩	n-án h-ái	boy
兄弟	x-i-ōng d-ì	brother
孩子	h-ái z-i	child（children 复数）
父亲	f-ù q-in	father
朋友	p-éng y-ǒu	friend
女孩	n-ǔ h-ái	girl
男人	n-án r-én	man
母亲	m-ǔ q-īn	mother
护士	h-ù sh-i	nurse
姐妹	j-iě m-èi	sister
女人	n-ǚ r-én	woman
医生	y-ī sh-ēng	doctor

2、家居及家庭生活用品 Housing and Household Items

床	ch-u-áng	bed	铃铛	l-íng d-āng	bell
瓶子	p-íng z-i	bottle	盒子	h-é z-i	box
椅子	y-ǐ z-i	chair	闹钟	n-ào zh-ōng	clock
电脑	d-i-àn n-ǎo	computer	茶杯	ch-á b-ēi	cup
碗橱	w-ǎn ch-ú	cupboard	书桌	sh-ū zh-u-ō	desk
门	m-én	doo	水壶	sh-uǐ h-ú	kettle
钥匙	y-ào sh-i	key	窗	ch-u-āng	window
小刀	x-i-ǎo d-āo	knife	灯	d-ēng	lamp
烤箱	k-ǎo x-i-āng	oven	盘子	p-án z-i	plate

48

房间	f-áng j-i-ān	room	架子	j-i-à z-i	shelf
汤勺	t-āng sh-áo	spoon	桌子	zh-u-ō z-I	table
雨伞	y-ǔ s-ǎn	umbrella	墙	q-i-áng	wall
电视机	d-i-àn sh-ì j-ī	television
电冰箱	d-i-àn b-īng x-i-āng	refrigerator
厨房	ch-ú f-áng	kitchen
玻璃杯	b-ō l-í b-ēi	glass

3、学习用品及玩具 School Supplies and Toys

书包	sh-ū b-āo	bag	书	sh-ū	book
风筝	f-ēng zh-ēng	kite	地图	d-ì t-ú	map
笔	b-ǐ	pen	铅笔	q-i-ān b-ǐ	pencil
玩具	w-án j-ù	toy

4、交通工具 Transportation vehicles

自行车	z-ì x-íng ch-ē	bike	船	ch-u-án	boat
飞机	f-ēi j-ī	plane	轮船	l-ún ch-u-án	ship
火车	huǒ ch-ē	train	卡车	kǎ ch-ē	truck
公共汽车	g-ōng g-òng q-ì ch-ē bus

5、身体部位 Body Parts

背	b-èi	back	眼睛	y-ǎn j-īng	eye
耳朵	ěr duo	ear	脸	l-i-ǎn	face
脚	j-i-ǎo	foot	头发	t-óu f-a	hair
手	sh-ǒu	hand	头	t-óu	head
膝盖	x-ī gài	knee	腿	t-uǐ	leg
嘴唇	z-uǐ ch-ún	lip	嘴巴	z-uǐ b-a	mouth
脖子	b-ó z-i	neck	鼻子	b-í z-i	nose
牙齿	y-á ch-ǐ	tooth（teeth 复数）

6、自然界 Nature

| 空气 | k-ōng q-ì | air | 云 | y-ún | cloud |
| 地球 | d-ì q-iú | earth | 草 | c-ǎo | grass |

月亮	y-uè l-i-àng	moon	雨	y-ǔ	rain
河	h-é	river	玫瑰	m-éi g-uì	rose
海	h-ǎi	sea	天空	t-i-ān k-ōng	sky
雪	x-uě	snow	声音	sh-ēng y-īn	sound
星星	x-īng x-ing	star	太阳	t-ài y-áng	sun
树	sh-ù	tree	声音	sh-ēng y-īn	voice
水	sh-ǔi	water	风	f-ēng	wind

7、场所、地点 Locations and Sites

乡村，国家	x-i-āng c-ūn g-u-ō j-i-ā	country
学院，大学	x-ué y-u-àn d-à x-ué	college
小屋	x-i-ǎo w-ū	cottage
花园	h-u-ā y-u-án	garden
大厅	d-à t-īng	hall
家	j-i-ā	home
屋	w-ū	house
公园	g-ōng y-u-án	park
道路	d-ào l-ù	road
学校	x-ué xiào	school
商店	sh-āng d-i-àn	store
街道	j-iē d-ào	street
村庄	c-ūn zh-u-āng	village
动物园	d-òng wù y-u-án	zoo

8、各种颜色 Colours

黑色	h-ēi s-è	black	蓝色	l-án s-è	blue
棕色	z-ōng s-è	brown	绿色	l-ǜ s-è	green
红色	h-óng s-è	red	白色	b-ái s-è	white
黄色	h-u-áng s-è	yello			
橘黄色	j-ú h-u-áng s-è	orange			

粉红色　　　f-ěn h-óng s-è　　　pink

9、衣物名称 Clothes

靴子	x-uē z-i	boot
帽子	m-ào z-i	cap
外衣	w-ài y-ī	coat
女服；童装	n-ǔ f-ú	dress
	t-óng zh-u-āng	
手套	sh-ǒu t-ào	glove
帽子	m-ào z-i	hat
凉鞋	l-i-áng x-ié	sandal
围巾	w-éi j-īn	scarf
衬衫	ch-èn sh-ān	shirt
短裤	d-u-ǎn k-ù	shorts
鞋	x-ié	shoe
裙子	q-ún z-i	skirt
短袜	d-u-ǎn w-à	sock
领带	l-ǐng d-ài	tie

10、蔬菜 、水果 、食品 Vegetables, Fruits and food

苹果	p-íng g-u-ǒ	apple
香蕉	x-i-āng j-i-āo	banana
豆子	d-òu z-i	bean
牛肉	n-iú r-òu	beef
面包	m-i-àn b-āo	bread
奶油	n-ǎi y-óu	butter
蛋糕	d-àn g-āo	cake
薯条	sh-ǔ t-i-áo	chip
咖啡	k-ā f-ēi	coffee
鸡蛋	j-ī d-àn	egg
果酱	g-u-ǒ j-i-àng	jam
牛奶	n-iú n-ǎi	milk

肉	r-òu	meat
橘子	j-ú z-i	orange
桃子	t-áo z-i	peach
梨子	l-í z-i	pear
米饭	m-ǐ f-àn	rice
糖果	t-áng g-u-ǒ	sweets

11、动物名称 Animals

熊	x-i-óng	bear
鸟	n-i-ǎo	bird
虫子	ch-ong z-i	bug
骆驼	l-u-ò t-u-o	camel
猫	m-āo	cat
小鸡	x-i-ǎo j-ī	chicken
牛	n-iú	cow
公鸡	g-ōng j-ī	cock
狗	g-ǒu	dog
鸭	y-ā	duck
象	x-i-àng	elephant
鱼	y-ú	fish
山羊	sh-ān y-áng	goat
母鸡	m-ǔ j-ī	hen
马	m-ǎ	horse
熊猫	x-i-óng m-āo	panda
猪	zh-ū	pig
兔	t-ù	rabbit
老鼠	l-ǎo sh-ǔ	rat
绵羊	m-i-án y-áng	sheep
老虎	l-ǎo h-ǔ	tiger
狼	l-áng	wolf

12、形容词与副词 Adjectives and Adverbs

大&小	d-à& x-i-ǎo	big & small
好&坏	h-ǎo & h-u-ài	good & bad
伤心&高兴	sh-āng x-īn & g-āo x-ìng	sad & glad
狂&疯	k-u-áng & f-ēng	crazy & mad
高&矮	g-āo & ǎi	tall & short
冷&热	l-ěng & r-è	cold & hot
忙碌&清闲	m-áng l-ù& q-īng x-i-án	busy & free
胖&瘦	p-àng & sh-òu	fat & thin
老&新	l-ǎo & x-īn	old & new
左&右	z-u-ǒ & y-òu	left & right
快的&慢的	k-u-ài d-e & m-àn d-e	fast & slow
早的&晚的	z-ǎo d-e & w-ǎn d-e	early & late
清洁&肮脏	q-īng j-i-é& āng z-āng	clean & dirty
容易&难	r-óng y-ì& n-án	easy & hard
对&错	d-uì& c-u-ò	right & wrong

13、动词 Verbs

看、看见	k-àn k-àn j-i-àn	look、 see
读、写	d-ú x-iě	read、 write
问、答	w-èn d-á	ask、 answer
跑、走	p-ǎo z-ǒu	run 、 walk
吃、喝	ch-ī h-ē	eat、 drink
坐、站	z-u-ò zh-àn	sit 、 stand
来、去	l-ái q-ù	come、 go
唱、跳	ch-àng t-i-ào	sing 、 dance
穿、穿上	ch-u-ān ch-u-ān sh-àng	wear 、 put on
爱、恨	ài h-èn	love 、 hate
照耀、闪烁	zh-ào y-ào sh-ǎn sh-u-ò	shine 、 twinkle
笑、哭	x-i-ào k-ū	smile、 cry
工作、学习	g-ōng z-u-ò x-ué x-í	work、 study
玩、学	w-án x-ué	play、study

第二课　　句子的拼读练习

Lesson Two　　Spelling Practice of the Sentences

1.你　好！N-ǐ h-ǎo!	Hello!
2.早晨好！Z-ǎo ch-én h-ǎo!	Good morning!
3.下午好！X-i-à w-ǔ h-ǎo！	Good afternoon!
4.晚上好！W-ǎn sh-àng h-ǎo!	Good evening!
5.晚　安！W-ǎn ān!	Good night!
6.你好吗？N-ǐ h-ǎo ma?	How are you?
7.很好，谢谢！Hěn h-ǎo,x-iè x-ie!	Fine, thanks!
8.再　见！Z-ài j-i-àn　！	Good bye!
9.回头见！H-uí t-óu j-i-àn!	See you later!
10.祝你好运! Zh-ù n-ǐ h-ǎo y-ùn!	Good luck!
11 新年快乐！X-īn n-i-án k-u-ài l-è .	Happy New Year!
12.现在几点了？X-i-àn z-ài j-ǐ d-i-ǎn l-e？	What time is it?
13.你是谁？N-ǐ sh-ì sh-uí　？	Who is that?
14.稍　等！Sh-āo d-ěng！	Hold on, please!
15.对不起。D-uì b-ù q-ǐ .	I am sorry.
16.没关系。M-éi g-u-ān x-ì.	That is OK.
17.祝贺你。Zh-ù h-è n-ǐ　.	Congratulations.
18.太遗憾了！T-ài y-í h-àn l-e！	What a pity!
19.祝你生日快乐！Zh-ù n-ǐ sh-ēng r-ì k-u-ài l-è!	Happy birthday!
20.认识你很高兴 R-èn sh-i n-ǐ h-ěn g-āo x-ing.	Glad to meet you!
21.你叫什么名字？N-ǐ j-i-ào sh-én m-e m-íng z-i.	What is your name?
22.我叫韩梅梅。W-ǒ j-i-ào h-án m-éi m-ei.	My name is Han Meimei.
23.你需要帮助吗？N-ǐ x-ū y-ào b-āng zh-ù m-a？	Can I help you?

24.我想买一本书。W-ǒ x-i-ǎng m-ǎi y-ī b-ěn sh-ū.　　　　I want a book.

25.这本书多少钱？Zh-è b-ěn sh-ū d-u-ō sh-ǎo q-i-án.　　　How much is the book?

26.今天天气如何？J-īn t-i-ān t-i-ān q-ì r-ú h-é?　　What is the weather like today?

27.今天有雨。　J-īn t-i-ān y-óu y-ǔ.　　　　　　　　It is rainy today.

28.明天你有空吗？M-íng t-i-ān n-ǐ y-ǒu k-òng m-a?　　Are you free tomorrow?

29.你好！我是韩梅梅！　N-ǐ h-ǎo! w-ǒ sh-ì h-án m-éi m-ei?

　　　　　　　　　　　　　　　Hello! This is Han Meimei speaking.

30.现在是上午9点钟。X-i-àn z-ài sh-ì sh-àng w-ǔ j-iǔ d-i-ǎn zh-ō-ng.

　　　　　　　　　　　　　　　It is nine o'clock now .

第三课：中国成语

Lesson Three   China Idoms

1 .   bàn tú   ér   fèi

半　途　而　废

You use the idiom 半途而废；to say that someone aban-dons a job they are doing half way;wasted.

2.   bù chǐ xià wèn

不　耻　下　问

If you describe a person as 不耻下问；you mean that when they do not know anything,they do not mind seeking the views of those junior to them.

3.   bù láo ér huò

不　劳　而　获

You use the idiom 不劳而获；to mean that someone who has not

worked for something has benefited from the fruit of labour of others.

4.   dǎ cǎo jīng shé

打　草　惊　蛇

The literal mean of 打草惊蛇；is 'to beat the grass and dis-turb the snake hiding in it'.This idiom is often used with words such as 不要，别，免得 to caution people that they have to execute an action discrteetly so as not to rouse others,especially their opponents.

5.   dé guò qiě guò

得　过　且　过

If you describe a person as 得过且过；you mean that they lack ambition and just want to muddle along in life.

6 .   dōng shān zài   qǐ

东 山 再 起

The idiom 东山再起 ；means to make a comeback.

7．fā yáng guāng dà

发 扬 光 大

The idiom 发扬光大 ;means to improve on the convention- always or skills of doing something and to popularize in further.

8．guāng míng zhèng dà

光 明 正 大

A person who is described as 光明正大 ； is upright and selfless.

9．hài qún zhī mǎ

害 群 之 马

A person who is said to be 害群之马 ；brings disrepute to the whole group;the black sheep of a family.

10．huā yán qiǎo yǔ

花 言 巧 语

The idiom 花言巧语 ; is sweet talk. The words may be mu-sic to your ears but they are insincere and intended to de-ceive you.

11．jiā yù hù xiǎo

家 喻 户 晓

The idiom 家喻户晓 ； means a household name.

12．jiàn yì yǒng wéi

见 义 勇 为

A person who is said to be 见义勇为 will not hesitate to help those in need; a Good Samaritan.

13．jǐng jǐng yǒu tiáo

井 井 有 条

If you say something is 井井有条 , it is in an orderly man-ner;shipshape.

14 ． liáng yào kǔ kǒu

良 药 苦 口

The idiom 良药苦口 literally means that medicine that cures often leaves a bitter taste in the mouth.It is often used now to mean that good advice is never pleasant to listen to.

15 ． míng luò sūn shān

名 落 孙 山

You use 名落孙山 to mean that a person has failed an exam.

16 ． pāo zhuān yǐn yù

抛 砖 引 玉

You use the idiom 抛砖引玉 to mean, modestly, that your view is view ordinary.You make a suggestion with the in-tention of eliciting greater ideas from others.

17 ． qíng tóng shǒu zú

情 同 手 足

When two men or boys are said to be 情同手足, they are best friends behaving like brothers.

18 ． sān sī ér xíng

三 思 而 行

The idiom 三思而行 means think twice or look before you leap.

19 ． shì bàn gōng bèi

事 半 功 倍

If what you do is described as 事半功倍,which means achive maximum results with little effort.

20 ． shǒu zhū dài tù

首 株 待 兔

When you describe someone as 守株待兔 , you mean that they are trying to gain something without doing anything.

21 ． shuǐ luò shí chū

水　落　石　出

The idiom 水落石出 is often used to mean that the whole incident is now clear.If you say 查个水落石出，you mean to get into the bottom of something to find out the reasons or causes.

22 . tóng gān gòng kǔ

同　甘　共　苦

The idiom 同甘共苦 means to stick together whatever the situation may be.

23 . wēn gù zhī xīn

温　故　知　新

The idiom 温故知新 means when you go over things you have already learnt,you will uncover new things or new knowledge.

24 . xìng zāi lè huò

幸　灾　乐　祸

A person who is described as 幸灾乐祸 delights in the misfortunes of others.

25 . xiù shǒu páng guān

袖　手　旁　观

The idiom 袖手旁观 means to stand there without lending a helping hand.

26 . yǐ shēn zuò zé

以　身　作　则

The idiom 以身作则 means to set an example for others to follow.

27 . yǐn shuǐ sī yuán

饮　水　思　源

You use 饮水思源 to refer to people who are grateful to others who have helped them to succeed.

28 . zài jiē zài lì

再　接　再　厉

You use 再接再厉 to refer to people who never say die.They always persever with a task even though they may have failed several times already.

29 . zhí   mí   bú   wù

执   迷   不   悟

People who are said to be 执迷不悟 are stubborn and re-use to recognize that what they are doing or believing is wrong.

30 . zhì tong   dào   hé

志   同   道   合

When you describe people as 志同道合, you mean that they have the same ambitions and share similar objectives or values.

第四章 如何学习写汉字
Section Four   How to write the Chinese Characters

1.Traditional characters & simplified characters

Traditional Chinese characters (fan ti zi) and simplified Chinese characters (jian ti zi) refer to the two standard sets of Chinese characters .

Traditional Chinese characters have been used throughout the Chinese history and now are officially used in the following districts of China , Taiwan, Hong Kong,Macau, and are most commonly used in overseas Chinese communities other than Singapore and Malaysia .

Simplified Chinese characters, which were derived from traditional Chinese characters and introduced by the government of the People's Republic of China in the 1950s ,are used in mainland China ,Singapore and Malaysia in official publications.

2.How to input the characters

If you feel writing Chinese characters with a pen is hard ,try inputting them using your computer keyboard and printing them out .

To add Keyboard/Input Method Editor (IME) in Win XP, see:

http://www.microsoft.com/globaldev/hand son/user/xpintlsupp.mspx#E4

When the Microsoft Pinyin IME is added, you will find it in the language bar at the right bottom corner of the screen as shown below .

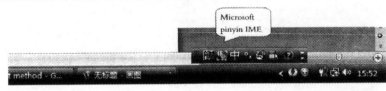

To input Chinese characters or words   ,simply   type   their pronunciations .Here   are   some examples .

要输入汉字或者汉语词语，只需键入它

1、繁体字和简体字

繁体字(fán tǐ zì)和简体字(jǎn tǐ zì) ,繁体字和简体字分别指汉字的两套标准字体。

繁体字是历史上中国人一致使用的字体，现在中国的台湾、香港、澳门地区和除新加坡、马来西亚外的大多数海外华人社会使用。

简体字是从繁体字简化而来的，由中华人民共和国政府在 20 世纪 50 年代开始倡导使用，现在在中国大陆通用，新加坡和马来西亚的官方出版物上使用。

2、如何将汉字输入电脑

要是你觉得用笔写汉字很累，就尝试用电脑键盘将汉字输入电脑并打印出来吧。

如何在 win XP 中增加输入法见：

http://www.microsoft.com/globald ev/handson/user/xpintlsupp.mspx#E4

微软拼音输入法增加好后，会在电脑屏幕右下角的语言栏处出现。见下图

们的拼音。具体例子见下图。

ren

1人 2任 3饪 4仁 5认 6忍 7刃 8壬 9韧 ◀▶

shenme

1什么 2深 3身 4椮 5申 6肾 7甚 8沈 9审 ◀▶

jiaotongdaxue

1交通大学 2交通 3绞痛 4交 5教 6叫 7较 ◀▶

Choose the characters or words below their pinyin and the input is completed.

然后选择拼音下方跳出的横框中你要的字或词便

可以了。

Similar method can be used on your mobile phone if it supports Chinese input.

如果你的手机支持汉字输入，你也可以用类似的

输入法在手机中输入汉字。

3. How to write the characters

如何书写汉字

1. Basic strokes

基本笔画

Number	Stroke	Name	Example	Number	Stroke	Name	Example
1	一	héng	女	10	丿	piě	八
2	⁊	héng zhé	四	11	㇄	piě zhé	幺
3	⁊	héng gōu	你	12	㇁	piě diǎn	女
4	⁊	héng piě	友	13	㇏	nà	人
5	丨	shù	十	14	丶	diǎn	六
6	亅	shù gōu	东	15	㇀	tí	给
7	丨	shù tí	以	16	㇉	wān gōu	子
8	ㄴ	shù zhé	山	17	㇂	xié gōu	我
9	㇄	shù wān	四	18	㇃	wò gōu	心

62

2. Rules of stroke orders in general （基本笔顺）：

1) From top to bottom （从上到下）：

一 二 三

2) From left to right （从左到右）：

丿 八

3) Horizontal before vertical （先横后竖）：

一 十

4) Middle before sides （先中间后两边）：

亅 小 小

5) From outside to inside （先外后内）：

丿 刀 月 月

6) Inside before sealing the box （先外后内再封口）：

丨 冂 回 四 四

7) Box before the cutting stroke （先写框再写穿过框的竖笔）：

丨 冂 口 中

8) Cutting stroke before the last horizontal stroke （先横后竖最后一横笔）：

一 二 干 王

3. Make it a try—writing the numbers （试写十个数字）：

one yī   two èr   three sān   four sì   five wǔ

six liù   seven qī   eight bā   nine jiǔ   ten shí

一									
一	一	一	一	一	一				

63

二 二

| 二 | 二 | 二 | 二 | 二 | | | | | | | |

三 三 三

| 三 | 三 | 三 | 三 | 三 | | | | | | | |

冂 冂 冂 四 四

| 四 | 四 | 四 | 四 | 四 | | | | | | | |

丁 五 五 五

| 五 | 五 | 五 | 五 | 五 | | | | | | | |

亠 六 六 六

| 六 | 六 | 六 | 六 | 六 | | | | | | | |

七 七

| 七 | 七 | 七 | 七 | 七 | | | | | | | |

八 八

| 八 | 八 | 八 | 八 | 八 | | | | | | | |

九 九

| 九 | 九 | 九 | 九 | 九 | | | | | | | |

4 New radicals and characters　　　　　　　　新部首和新汉字

rén　person

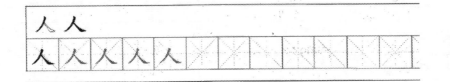

radical form（when appearing
at the left side of a character）

name:　　　dānrénpáng
　　　　　　单人旁

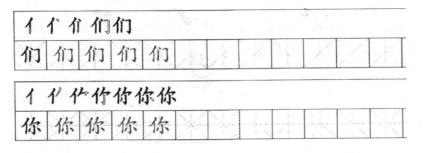

65

female　　　　nǚ

radical form（when appearing
left side of a character）
name：　*nǚ zì páng*
　　　　　女字旁

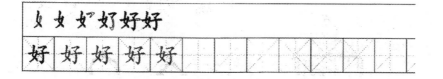

好	好	好	好	好					

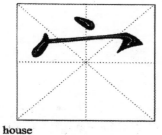

house
radical form（appearing on
top of a character）

name：　　　　*bǎogàitóu*
　　　　　　　宝盖头

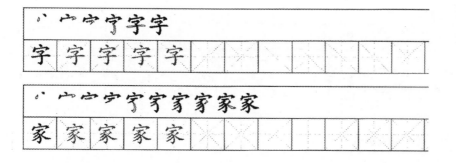

字	字	字	字	字					

家	家	家	家	家					

fire   huǒ

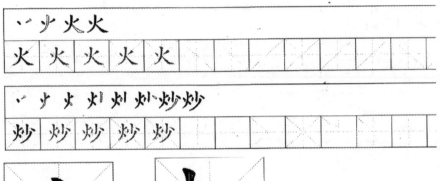

丶 丷 火 火

火	火	火	火	火							

丶 丷 火 灯 灼 炒 炒 炒

炒	炒	炒	炒	炒							

earth, soil   tǔ   radical form（when appearing at
the left side of a character）

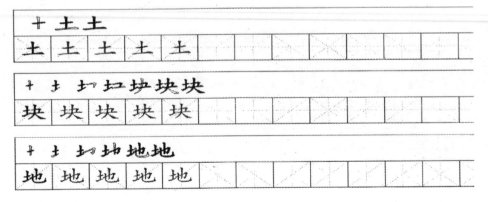

十 土 土

土	土	土	土	土						

十 土 圸 圹 块 块 块

块	块	块	块	块						

十 土 圸 地 地 地

地	地	地	地	地						

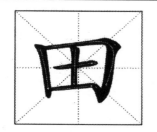

field　　　　tián

门 冂 用 田 田

| 田 | 田 | 田 | 田 | 田 | | | | | | | |

冂 冂 曰 甲 甲 里 里

| 里 | 里 | 里 | 里 | 里 | | | | | | | |

冂 冂 用 田 田 罗 男 男

| 男 | 男 | 男 | 男 | 男 | | | | | | | |

crops　　　　hé　　　radical form（when appearing at
　　　　　　　　　　　.the left side of a character）

二 千 千 禾 禾

| 禾 | 禾 | 禾 | 禾 | 禾 | | | | | | |

二 千 千 禾 禾 和 和 和

| 和 | 和 | 和 | 和 | 和 | | | | | | |

二 千 千 禾 禾 香 香 香 香

| 香 | 香 | 香 | 香 | 香 | | | | | | |

二 千 千 禾 禾 和 和 种 种

| 种 | 种 | 种 | 种 | 种 | | | | | | |

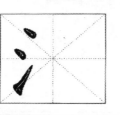

water   shuǐ   radical form (when appearing at the left side of a character)

name: sān diǎn shuǐ
三点水

ice   bīng   radical form (when appearing at the left side of a character)

name: liǎng diǎn shuǐ
两点水

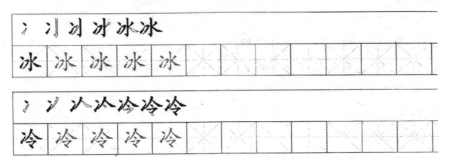

gold, metal   jīn

radical form（when appearing at
the left side of a character）
name: jīn zì páng
               金字旁

丿𠂉𠂉𠂉𠂉𠂉𠂉钅钅钅钅钅钱钱钱钱

| 钱 | 钱 | 钱 | 钱 | 钱 | | | | | | | | | |

丿𠂉𠂉𠂉钅钅钅钅钅钅钅银银银

| 银 | 银 | 银 | 银 | 银 | | | | | | | | | |

丿𠂉𠂉𠂉钅钅钅钅钅钟钟

| 钟 | 钟 | 钟 | 钟 | 钟 | | | | | | | | | |

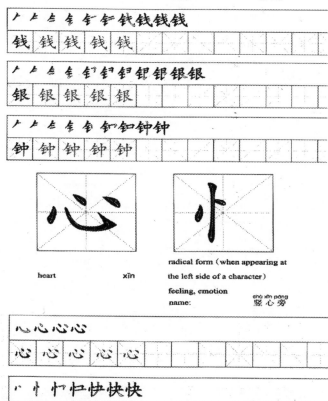

heart   xīn

radical form（when appearing at
the left side of a character）
feeling, emotion
name: shù xīn páng
               竖心旁

心心心心

| 心 | 心 | 心 | 心 | 心 | | | | | | | | | |

丶忄忄忄快快快

| 快 | 快 | 快 | 快 | 快 | | | | | | | | | |

丶忄忄忄忄忄忄慢慢慢慢慢慢

| 慢 | 慢 | 慢 | 慢 | 慢 | | | | | | | | | |

丶忄忄忙忙忙

| 忙 | 忙 | 忙 | 忙 | 忙 | | | | | | | | | |

sun, day　　　　　rì

丿	冂	日	日						
日	日	日	日	日					

丿	冂	日	日	明	明	明	明		
明	明	明	明	明					

丿	冂	日	日	昨	昨	昨	昨	昨	
昨	昨	昨	昨	昨					

walk, move

radical form (appearing at the left side

and bottom of a character)

name: 走之底

二 丰 元 远 远 远 远

| 远 | 远 | 远 | 远 | 远 | | | | | | | |

厂 斤 斤 斤 近 近 近

| 近 | 近 | 近 | 近 | 近 | | | | | | | |

一 ア 不 不 还 还 还

| 还 | 还 | 还 | 还 | 还 | | | | | | | |

丶 一 ナ 文 文 这 这 这

| 这 | 这 | 这 | 这 | 这 | | | | | | | |

hand   shŏu

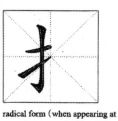

radical form (when appearing at

the left side of a character)

name: 提手旁

二 三 手 手

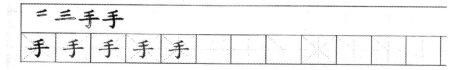

| 手 | 手 | 手 | 手 | 手 | | | | | | |

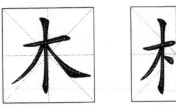 

wood　　　mù　　　radical form (when appearing at
　　　　　　　　　　the left side of a character)

十 才 木 木

| 木 | 木 | 木 | 木 | 木 | | | | | | | |

十 才 才 才 札 杯 杯

| 杯 | 杯 | 杯 | 杯 | 杯 | | | | | | | |

十 才 才 机 机 机

| 机 | 机 | 机 | 机 | 机 | | | | | | | |

十 才 才 杧 朾 板 板 板

| 板 | 板 | 板 | 板 | 板 | | | | | | | |

moon, month　　　yuè

几 月 月 月

| 月 | 月 | 月 | 月 | 月 | | | | | | | |

十 艹 艹 甘 苴 其 其 期 期 期 期 期

| 期 | 期 | 期 | 期 | 期 | | | | | | | |

几 月 月 朋 朋 朋 朋 朋

| 朋 | 朋 | 朋 | 朋 | 朋 | | | | | | | |

口

enclosure（enclosing a character）

name: *guó zi kuàng*
国字框

冂 冂 冈 冈 冈 园 园

| 园 | 园 | 园 | 园 | 园 | | | | | | | |

冂 冂 冂 冈 国 国 国 国

| 国 | 国 | 国 | 国 | 国 | | | | | | | |

冂 冂 冈 冈 因 因

| 因 | 因 | 因 | 因 | 因 | | | | | | | |

丝   纟

silk   *sī*   radical form（when appearing at the left side of a character）

name：*jiǎo sī páng*
绞丝旁

纟 纟 纟 丝 丝

| 丝 | 丝 | 丝 | 丝 | 丝 | | | | | | | |

纟 纟 纟 红 红 红

| 红 | 红 | 红 | 红 | 红 | | | | | | | |

纟 纟 纟 纟 纱 纱 给 给 给

| 给 | 给 | 给 | 给 | 给 | | | | | | | |

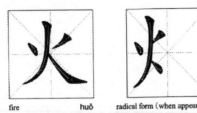

fire   huǒ   radical form (when appearing at the
left side of a character)

冂 冈 冈 囗 甲 甲 黒 黒 黑 黑 黑 黑

黑	黑	黑	黑	黑					

十 才 扌 执 执 热 热 热 热

热	热	热	丝	丝					

heart   xīn   radical form (when appearing at the
bottom of a character)
feeling,emotion

一 乍 乍 乍 乍 怎 怎 怎 怎

怎	怎	怎	怎	怎					

十 才 才 木 相 相 相 相 想 想 想 想

想	想	想	想	想					

亻 亻 仵 佟 佟 你 你 您 您 您 您

您	您	您	您	您					

冂 冂 用 田 思 思 思 思

思	思	思	思	思					

speech   yán   radical form（when appearing at the

left side of a character）

name: *yán zì páng*

言字旁

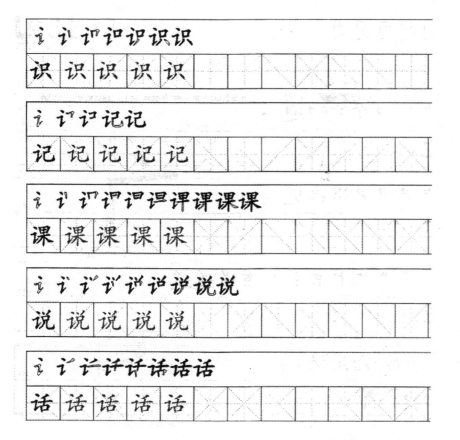

讠	讠	识	识	识	识	识						
识	识	识	识	识								

讠	讠	记	记	记								
记	记	记	记	记								

讠	讠	识	识	识	识	课	课	课				
课	课	课	课	课								

讠	讠	讠	讠	识	识	识	说	说				
说	说	说	说	说								

讠	讠	讠	讠	讠	话	话	话					
话	话	话	话	话								

广

wide;dwelling
（radical meaning） guǎng

一 广 广											
广	广	广	广	广							

一 广 广 庐 庐 店 店 店											
店	店	店	店	店							

一 广 广 广 广 应 应 座 座 座											
座	座	座	座	座							

厂

factory;cliff, dwelling
（radical meaning） chǎng

厂 厂											
厂	厂	厂	厂	厂							

厂 厂 斤 斤											
斤	斤	斤	斤	斤							

厂 厂 斤 斤 斤 厢 厢 厢 厢 厢											
厢	厢	厢	厢	厢							